THE STRANGER NOTES

LIFE OF CAMUS

Albert Camus was born November 7, 1913, and reared in Algeria, a country exposed to the blistering African sun and the plain by the Mediterranean sea. These roots—the sun and the sea—have spread into all of Camus' writings—the novels, the plays, and the essays. They are a part of his lyricism, his symbolism, and his values. The universe, it seems from his early notebook, *(Noces)*, was mother, father, and lover for the young Camus, and from the first, Camus was aware of the paradoxical aspects of his natural world. The sensual free pleasure of swimming and hiking was in continuous contrast to the bare stony earth that made living a matter of poverty and destitution. He was early aware of the absurd condition of man's being totally alone in a resplendent universe. This concept is Camus' equivalent of "In the beginning. . . ." Against its truth, all of his writings sound revolt, for he refused to be deceived by social religious or individual submissions that ignored or defied the irreducible truth that man alone is responsible for himself, his meaning, and his measure. Camus' writings are a testament to a continuing belief in man's exiled but noble condition.

Lucien Camus, Albert's father, was killed in 1914 during World War I's Battle of the Marne, and the year-old child was reared by his deaf mother. She had little money and was apparently a rather joyless and boring companion for her son. It is little wonder that he spent much of his time with athletics, studies, and necessary part-time employment. When he finished school, a university degree seemed the most important challenge available to a poverty-stricken student. Camus was enthusiastic and ambitious about his studies, but he was not able to complete them immediately. In 1930, while he was a student of philosophy at the University of Algiers, he almost died during a bout with tuberculosis, an illness which would periodically afflict him for many years. Then, after his recovery, he was beset by the constant problem of poverty and was forced to support himself for several years as a meteorologist, a police clerk, and a salesman. During this time he married and divorced and also joined and left the Communist party. In 1935, a year before he received his degree from the University, he founded The Workers' Theater, a group formed to present plays for Algiers' working population. Before his theater venture ended in 1939, Camus published *L'Envers et L'Endroit (Betwixt and Between)*, essays that deal with man and death in terms of an oblivious universe. They are mood pieces, written in Camus' mixture of irony and lyricism, describing man's defenselessness and his isolation in a splendid universe whose only rule for man seems to be death. Yet there is an optimism in these essays; it is here that Camus first advocates living *as if* man had eternal value. He believes that only in man's courageous rebellion to confront himself and his world can he begin to create a civilization that can rescue itself from a nihilistic catastrophe.

Between the years 1937 and 1939, Camus wrote book reviews and occasional essays for the *Algier-Republicain*, a left-wing newspaper. Later he assumed the editorship of the *Soir-Republicain*, but for only a short time. He was severely critical of the French colonial government and after the newspaper folded, he soon found himself unofficially unwelcome and unable to find a job in the country. Thus in 1940 he left Algeria and went to live in Paris. There he worked for a time with the *Paris-Soir*, but his journalistic career was once again curtailed. This time the Germans had invaded France.

Camus returned once again to North Africa, where he remarried and began teaching in a private school in Oran. He continued to write and filled several notebooks with sketches and several versions of *The Stranger* and *The Myth of Sisyphus*, and he also worked on ideas for a new novel, *The Plague*.

A year later, both *The Stranger* and *The Myth of Sisyphus* were published, and Camus was established as a writer of international importance. *The Stranger*'s Meursault has now become a literary archetype, and the beginning sentences of *The Stranger* have become synonymous with an absurd or ironic situation. Never before had the public read about a man who was so absolutely honest as Meursault. In fact, his honesty is perhaps his only meritorious quality. Meursault is an anti-hero, an inconspicuous clerk who does not believe in God, but cannot lie. He does believe in going to the movies, swimming, and making love. He is finally beheaded because he murdered an Arab; he is condemned, however, because he seemed indifferent at his mother's funeral. Meursault becomes aware of his freedom and his happiness only after he is imprisoned, a situation similar to that of the imprisoned Oranian

THE STRANGER

Notes

including
Life of Camus
Camus and the Absurd
List of Characters
Critical Commentaries
Character Analyses
Review Questions
Selected Bibliography

by
Gary K. Carey, M.A.
University of Colorado

consulting editor
James L. Roberts, Ph.D.
Department of English
University of Nebraska

Cliffs Notes
INCORPORATED
LINCOLN, NEBRASKA   68501

New Edition

ISBN   0-8220-1229-4

CONTENTS

citizens in *The Plague*. He faces death with sensitive and joyous awareness of his last moments and hopes for a vivid end and an angry shouting crowd as a witness.

In the year of *The Stranger*, 1942, Camus decided to return to France and commit himself to the French Resistance Movement. He enlisted in an organization known as Combat, also the title of the clandestine newspaper he edited during the Occupation. After Paris was liberated in 1944, Camus continued to edit *Combat* for four years while he published collections of his wartime essays. His plays, *The Misunderstanding* and *Caligula*, were presented during 1944; the latter was as well received as the former was not. In 1945, Camus toured the United States, lecturing and gathering firsthand impressions of the national power that was credited with ending the long war.

His allegory, *The Plague*, was published in June, 1947, and was immediately cited as a major literary work. The critics and the public were unanimous in their praise for this somberly narrated chronicle. As a popular book it had none of the formula gimmicks; it had no intense, romantic plot-line, no fascinating setting, nor even a powerfully drawn characterization of its main character. But to a nation recovering from an enemy occupation, it was an authentic account of months during which only human dignity and survival mattered. Postwar readers were appreciative and sympathetic to this writer who had faithfully, and not melodramatically, recorded the suffering and misery of separation and exile.

In 1949, upon his return to France from a South American tour, Camus became quite ill and went into almost total seclusion, only occasionally publishing collections of more of his political essays. In 1951, when he was recovered, he published an extensive study of metaphysical, historical, and artistic revolt, *The Rebel*. It was a controversial book and was responsible for breaking the friendship he had with Jean Paul Sartre.

After *The Rebel*, Camus began translating favorite works of international playwrights. His adaptions were rapidly produced and included Calderón's *La Devocion de la Cruz*, Larivey's *Les Espirits*, Buzzati's *Un Caso Clinico*, Faulkner's *Requiem for a Nun*, and others. More collections of his political essays appeared, plus many prefaces to contemporary writings.

In 1956, a new fictional work appeared, his novel *The Fall*. The book deals with a successful and admired lawyer who suddenly faces his conscience after he refuses to help a woman drowning in a suicide attempt. The confessions of his fraud and guilt contain precise and penetrating comments about contemporary society. It is not as ambitious or as lengthy as *The Plague*, but it is as polished a masterpiece as *The Stranger*.

The following year Camus was awarded the Nobel Prize for Literature, and two years later he was killed in an automobile accident on January 4, 1960. The many eulogistic essays which appeared afterward remarked on the absurdity of his death — its suddenness, its uselessness, and the lack of logic to explain why. Camus, however, was probably more aware of the significance of his individual life than any of his essayists: his meaningless death is the key witness to his body of literature.

CAMUS AND THE ABSURD

To enter into the literary world of Albert Camus, one must realize, first off, that one is dealing with an author who does not believe in God. Major characters in Camus' fiction, therefore, can probably be expected either to disbelieve or to wrestle with the problem of belief. One's first response then, as a reader, might profitably be a brief consideration of what might happen to a character who comes to realize that there is no Divinity, no God. What happens when he realizes that his death is final, that his joys, his disappointments, and his sufferings are brief flickers preluding an afterlife of nothingness? What changes in his daily pattern of work-eat-love-sleep must he now effect? Much like Kafka's Joseph K., the man in question has staggeringly comprehended that he is condemned to an eternal void — and because of no crime. Only because he is part of a meaningless birth-death cycle is he doomed; the fact of death and his mortality is all. He sees, in short, The End focused on the screen of his future, the screen on which he used to project his dreams and hopes. Hope based on anything superhuman is now futile. He sees an end for himself and his fellowmen. So, what then? Suicide, if all is meaningless? Or a blind return flight toward an external, though ever-silent God?

This concern with death and its abyss of nonexistence is the basis for most of Camus' literary works. Condemned to an everlasting zero of eternity, Camus' characters often suffer their author's own involvement and anguish; and, for his readers, the recognition of the fact of their own deaths is the starting point for their confronting and experiencing Camus' concept of the Absurd.

As a salvation, however, from despair and nihilism, Camus' Absurd embraces a positive optimism—optimism in the sense that much emphasis is placed on human responsibility for civilizing the world. The fictional characters, therefore, who shoulder their new *mortal* responsibility, are often characterized as rebels. In revolt from both a cowardly suicide and an equally cowardly flight from faith, the new optimism suggests man's returning to the center of a philosophical tightrope above an intensely physical death and, in his revolt, performing precariously. Above the threat of death, in confrontation with death, the metaphysical ropewalker acts "as if" his actions mattered. Obviously they do not in any long-range sense. And, rather than scamper to either the poles of Hope or Suicide, he knows that he will eventually fall, but stays mid-center. Obviously, his life, the lives of all men do not *finally* matter. Death is definitive. But, clown-like, he creates new acts, new entertainments—reaching, gesturing. Exploiting his precarious posture in a new burst of freedom, he restructures his actions, and in vivid contrast to death, he diffuses joy and a sense of ridiculous responsibility.

Walking on this razor's edge of "as if" means that man must act to his fellowmen as though life had meaning; in short, living an absurdity. Knowing that man has only man to depend upon, however, he can take fresh courage. He is now rid of fearful superstitions and questioning theories; he can now discard the religious faiths which assume that man is subservient to a Something divine and eternal. Man now has no excuse for failure, except himself. "God's will" as an excuse for failure is no longer valid. Man succeeds or fails because of the strength, or the lack of it, in himself. Camus challenges man to do the work which he has, too often, assigned to God.

LIST OF CHARACTERS

Meursault
The narrator, an Algerian clerk who is sentenced to death for murdering an Arab.

Céleste
Meursault's friend and owner of a restaurant where he usually dines.

Warden
In charge of the old age home in Marengo where Meursault's mother dies.

Gatekeeper
Inmate and employee in the same institution.

Pérez
Close friend of Meursault's mother at the old age home.

Marie Cardona
Meursault's mistress, formerly a typist and a stenographer in Meursault's office.

Emmanuel
Another worker in Meursault's office.

Salamano
Lives with his grotesque spaniel on Meursault's floor.

Raymond Sintès
Lives on the same floor, reputed to be a pimp.

"Robot-woman"
Woman who shares Meursault's table at Céleste's one day and later attends his trial.

Masson
Owner of the cottage at the beach visited by Raymond, Meursault, and Marie on the day of the murder; friend of Raymond.

Examining Magistrate
Conducts the preliminary interrogations.

CRITICAL COMMENTARIES

PART ONE

CHAPTER I

The Stranger is a very short novel, divided into two parts. In Part One, covering eighteen days, we witness a funeral, a love affair, and a murder. In Part Two, covering about a year, we are present at a trial that recreates those same eighteen days from various characters' memories and points of view. Part One is full of mostly insignificant days in the life of Meursault, an insignificant man, until he commits a murder; Part Two is an attempt, in a courtroom, to judge not only Meursault's crime but also to judge his life. Camus juxtaposes two worlds; Part One focuses on subjective reality; Part Two, on a more objective, faceted reality.

The novel opens with two of the most quoted sentences in existential literature: "Mother died today. Or, maybe, yesterday; I can't be sure." The impact of this indifference is shocking, yet it is a brilliant way for Camus to begin the novel. This admission of a son's unconcern about his mother's death is the key to Meursault's simple, uneventful life as a shipping clerk. He lives, he doesn't think too much about his day-to-day living, and now his mother is dead. And what does her death have to do with his life? To Meursault, life is not all that important; he doesn't ask too much of life, and death is even less important. He is content to, more or less, just exist. But by the end of the novel, he will have changed; he will have questioned his "existing" and measured it against "living"—living with an awareness that one can have and demand for himself—that is, a passion for life itself.

Today's readers of this novel have usually been exposed to such an anti-hero as Meursault, but to those who read this novel when it was first published, Meursault was a most unusual man. They were confronted with a man who has to attend to the details of a death—and not just a death, but the death of his mother. And the tone of what Meursault says is: so, she's dead. This tone is exactly what Camus wanted: he calculated on its shock value; he wanted his readers to examine closely this man who does not react as most of us are expected to do. Meursault is very matter-of-fact about his mother's death. He does not hate his mother; he is merely indifferent to her death. She lived in a nursing home not far from him because he didn't have enough money to pay the rent and buy food for them both, and also because she needed somebody to be with her a great deal of the time. They didn't see each other very often because, in Meursault's words, they had "nothing else to say to each other."

Camus is challenging us, in effect, with this idea: Meursault has a unique freedom; he does not have to react to death as we are taught by the church, by novels, movies, and cultural mores. His mother gave him birth; she reared him. Now he is an adult; he is no longer a child. Parents cannot remain "parents"; children, likewise, at a certain point, are no longer "children." They become adults, and when Meursault became an adult, he and his mother were no longer close. Eventually, they had "nothing else to say to each other." Meursault is no longer responsible to his mother for his actions. He defines himself and his own destiny. And, at this moment in his life, Meursault cannot succumb to the rituals of frantic, emotional breast-beating because of his mother's death. Meursault is not rebellious; he has simply discarded burdensome gestures. He cannot exaggerate his feelings.

Meursault has a special kind of freedom; he has made a commitment, an unconscious commitment, really; he has committed himself to living his life his way, even though it is dull, monotonous, and uneventful. He has no desire, no driving ambition, to prove his worth to other people. To most people, a funeral is an emotional trauma; for Meursault, note that his mother's wake is so insignificant that he borrows a black tie and armband for the funeral: why spend money for them when he would use them only one time? And he almost misses his bus for the funeral. He will bury his mother with church rites, but his sense of freedom is his own; he will physically do certain things, but he cannot express emotions which do not exist.

Thus we see Meursault's reaction to death. Consider, then, after the funeral, his attitude toward life. Meursault enjoys life. One can't say that he has a rage for living, but he affirms simple physical pleasures — swimming, friendships, and sex — not spectacularly, but remember that he is not a hero, just a simple shipping clerk. Note, too, that on the way to the funeral, during the vigil, and during the funeral itself, Meursault's reactions are mostly physical. When he enters the mortuary, for example, his attention is not on the wooden box that holds his mother's corpse. He notices, first, the skylight above and the bright, clean whitewashed walls. Even after the mortuary keeper has left, Meursault's attention is not on the coffin; instead, he reacts to the sun, "getting low, and the whole room was flooded with a pleasant, mellow light."

During the funeral procession, Meursault is not concerned with his mother's existence in an afterlife. She is dead; he is alive, and he is sweaty and hot, and doing what he is expected to do for a funeral, but these are all physical acts. Physically, he experiences the "blazing hot afternoon," the "sun-drenched countryside . . . dazzling," a "shimmer of heat," and he is "almost blinded by the glaze of light." This is what is painful to Meursault; he is not torn by religious agony or by a sense of loss. And besides Camus' showing us Meursault's physical responses to living, as opposed to his feelings about death, he is preparing us for the climax of Part One: Meursault's murder of the Arab. Again, the sun will be glaring, dazzling, and blinding; in fact, one of Meursault's defenses in court as to why he shot the Arab will be: "because of the sun."

In contrast to Meursault's reactions to the funeral and the heavy heat of the sun is Thomas Pérez. Old Pérez was a friend of Meursault's mother; they had a kind of romance. He follows the funeral procession, limping in the broiling sun, sometimes dropping so far behind that he has to take shortcuts to rejoin the procession. At the funeral, he faints.

Meursault, not Camus, tells us these facts. Meursault's narrative is documentary, objective, like a black-and-white photograph. He is not effusive when he tells us of Pérez's aged, wrinkled face and the tears streaming from his eyes. There is no attempt for sympathy. Meursault states facts, then tells us that his own thoughts are focused on getting back to Algiers and going to bed and sleeping for twelve hours.

Can we condemn Meursault? Should he have shed tears? Should he have thrown himself on his mother's casket? Or should we recognize his honesty? In Part Two, a jury will judge him and will find him guilty, not because he murdered an Arab, but mainly because he could not and did not weep at his mother's funeral. Shall we also condemn him? Camus says No; a man must be committed to himself, to his own values, and not be confined by certain value judgments of others. It is important to be a physical, *mortal* man, as opposed to being a half-man, living with the myth of someday becoming an immortal spirit.

Meursault's philosophy is, despite its unusual nature, very positive. He cannot live with illusions. He will not lie to himself. This life now is more important than living for a mythical then. When, according to Camus, one has seen the value of living with no illusion of an afterlife, he has begun to explore the world of the Absurd. Values must be, ultimately, self-defined, and certainly not by the church. Why fake an emotion because society says that it is proper etiquette? A lifetime is only so long and can end very suddenly. Camus would have us ask ourselves: why am I living a life that I have not structured? How old is the universe and who am I amidst the millions of people who are dead in the earth and the millions who are still living on this earth? There is no Holy One who cares about me; the whirling universe is alien, uncaring. Only *I* can try to determine my significance. Death is ever-present and, afterward, nothing. These are all questions and issues that Meursault, by the end of the novel, will have examined. He will have become an Absurd Man, and Camus has shown us the genesis of this philosophy in this opening chapter. Slowly, we will see how this rather simple shipping clerk will change, how he will gain immense insight into the importance of his life, and how he will learn to enjoy it passionately, ironically, as he faces death.

CHAPTER II

After showing us Meursault's reaction to death, Camus shows us a day during which Meursault reacts to life. Meursault wakes up and realizes how exhausting the funeral has been, physically. It would be nice to go swimming. There are no introspective feelings about his mother, about how she looked when she was alive, how she smiled, the expression in her eyes, the things which she and he talked about years ago, his childhood with her—or even her absence, forever. Right now, swimming would be pleasant.

By chance, on the swimming raft, Meursault meets a girl who worked for a short time in his office and they go to a film that night, a comedy of all things, and then they go home and have sex.

We have seen Meursault's casual reaction to his mother's death; now, we see him manage a casual pickup. Marie knows that Meursault's mother has just been buried because she asks him about his black tie, but she's unconcerned, for the most part. Note, too, that Meursault tells Marie that his mother "died yesterday." It's of so little importance to him that he confuses, absently, the day of her funeral with the day of her death. Today is Saturday. Meursault's mother died, probably, Wednesday or Thursday; she was buried "yesterday."

Next morning, Meursault awakens; it is Sunday. There is nothing very exciting or special about Sundays, except for the fact that he dislikes Sundays. He has awakened after having had sex with Marie, but he is not disappointed about Marie's not being there when he wakes up. And he does not tell us how satisfying their lovemaking was. Yet he is responsive to the smell of the salt from Marie's hair. He falls asleep again and, when he wakes again, he smokes in bed until midday.

Recall that on the bus, traveling to his mother's funeral, Meursault was so sleepy he could hardly keep his eyes open; in fact, he thinks he dozed off for a while. He lives rather like an animal; if he's sleepy, he dozes. Remember, too, that Meursault had fleeting guilt feelings about dozing off during the ordeal of the vigil and during the funeral itself, but today, he stays in bed because it is pleasant to lie there and smoke.

When Meursault does get up, he doesn't know what to do. He wanders around the apartment, reads an old newspaper, and cuts out an advertisement for a scrapbook that he keeps of amusing things. Then he goes out on the balcony. He is uneasy, unhappy on Sundays. Sundays are unstructured. Weekdays may be monotonous but there are certain things to do at certain times; Saturdays are for fun. But then comes Sunday, completely unstructured.

Depicting this kind of mechanical, day-to-day living is important for Camus' purpose. In his *Myth of Sisyphus,* he said that the discovery and the disgust of this monotony—"rising, tram, four hours in the office or the factory . . ."—is absolutely essential for an understanding of the Absurd. Meursault has not yet made this discovery, but Meursault is not, by nature, introspective; he likes small pleasures—sex, swimming, a good night's sleep, and smoking. He will eventually make his discovery about the meaningless routine of his life, but it will come later in the novel. For the present, Camus wants us to see Meursault's restlessness on a day when there is no routine—no "rising, tram, four hours in the office . . ."

When Meursault goes out on the balcony, he observes the people below him. Sundays, for them, seem to have a routine: young men going to the movies, a waiter sweeping sawdust, a tobacco seller bringing a chair out onto the pavement, and the empty streetcars going by. This has happened many Sundays. Meursault watches during the afternoon, he smokes, he watches the evening come, and then he eats some bread and macaroni. He says that he's "managed to see another Sunday through . . ." In a word, he is bored.

The tone of this chapter is, again, largely a tone of indifference, except that today Meursault enjoys smoking in bed and smelling the salt from Marie's hair on the pillow beside him. But read again the passage describing his perception of this Sunday afternoon. He is aware, even if passively, that the street lights reveal "little pools of brightness," that the lights of the streetcars shine, "lighting up a girl's hair, a smile, or a silver bangle"; the sky becomes "velvety black." These fragments of sensitivity might go almost unnoticed. Meursault enjoys basic pleasures, but he also has a poetic percep- tiveness within him—despite his passive reaction to his mother's death and his having had sex with Marie and his comment that "nothing had changed."

Yet what meaning has Meursault given to this Sunday? He has slept and smoked and sat on his balcony, and watched—alone. He is not deeply troubled about such things as—my life is wasted; I am bored; or I am lonely; in contrast, he has an ability to sit and watch, delighting, in small degrees, to colors, to the sky, and to the feel of the air. Meursault is not like an ordinary major character in a novel, and this "sitting and doing nothing" will be used in Part Two to condemn him. But one must still deal with the present, for this is what matters most to Meursault. Has Meursault done anything that has been especially enjoyable today? Has he chosen to make this day, in any way, significant, even in a small way, memorable? No. It has been just another Sunday and Meursault has "gotten through it." As he says, "It's all the same to me: makes no differ- ence much." Life. Death. He faces them with the same easy in- difference. Just as his mother's death was meaningless, so is his life, except for the few sensual pleasures and the fact that he lives the way he wants to. Meursault has yet to realize that he can make his life have meaning, that it can have intensity. Before that hap- pens, however, he must confront this monotonous, meaningless routine day-to-day living and be disgusted by the waste he has made of each day, even Sundays, in order to be liberated. When this awakening comes, it will shatter the drifting rhythm of his life. But Camus must show us, first, Meursault's going through the empty motions of living so that we will have a perspective of Meursault's realizing and becoming aware of the possibilities of what life can contain.

CHAPTER III

Camus moves us in this chapter through one of Meursault's work days. It opens on a Monday and there are references to the age of Meursault's mother. Meursault does not know how to answer when he is asked how old she was; it is a matter that never seemed of importance to him. But do not label Meursault a nihilist or a cynic. He is indifferent to his mother's age and he is probably ignorant of how old she really was. And he can't understand why his employer looks relieved when Meursault answers, without any knowledge, "round about sixty." Moreover, why his employer would ask such a question is a mystery to Meursault. He could have answered fifty, and he would have heard "how terrible; so young." Had he said that she was eighty, he would have heard, "well, she led a long life." The age of his mother is simply of no consequence to Meursault.

Note what Camus is doing here; he is showing us that Meursault, instead of bothering with deep guilt about not knowing his mother's age, is annoyed. And, in contrast, he is happy and enjoys the physical pleasure of washing his hands at work and he enjoys this act less at the end of the day because the roller towel is sopping wet. This small act is what is important to Meursault. In fact, he has mentioned this business of the soggy towel to his employer, who considers it a mere detail; to Meursault, the age of his mother is a "mere detail."

In the same way that Meursault, rather impulsively, thought that swimming would be pleasant, after leaving work for a lunch break, he and another employee, Emmanuel, pause a moment to look at the sea, an ever-fascinating phenomenon for Meursault; they endure the "scorching hot" sun for a moment, then decide to do something irrational; they run, half-dazed by the heat, and madly jump onto a big firetruck coming toward them. They achieve a small goal, a fun game, following a child's instinct to dare to do something wild and sudden. What they accomplish makes them feel proud. Who else that afternoon decided to run and jump on a fast-moving firetruck? Probably only Meursault and Emmanuel. This is another facet of Meursault's uniqueness; his job as a shipping clerk may be dull, but, spontaneously, he acts without thinking, doing something which is both physical and satisfying.

After a nap and a cigarette, Meursault endures the rest of the afternoon in an office that is "stifling," making his slow, cool evening stroll home even more satisfying; again, Camus focuses on Meursault's physical reactions rather than on an introspective analysis about himself or his relationship with Marie or with his mother.

There is a bit of black humor injected into the novel when Meursault reaches his apartment. A neighbor of his, Salamano, and a dog also lead a routine life. But, unlike Meursault's life, which is usually solitary, Salamano is, as it were, almost married in a love/hate relationship with his dog. And, Meursault tells us, they resemble one another (hairless, scabby, and hunched up) and, most important, they seem to fiercely detest one another.

This routine of living together has lasted eight years, the dog being walked regularly and beaten regularly. This does not particularly matter to Meursault; they are merely a curious couple of neighbors. Unlike Meursault, Raymond Sintès, an acquaintance of Meursault's, is disgusted by Salamano's living eight years with his dog—loving him, hating him, and beating him. But not Meursault. Salamano and his dog choose to live that way; otherwise, the dog would run away. At any rate, it would be ridiculous to worry a lot or try to solve a situation that has lasted eight years.

A rebel, without knowing or caring about being one, Meursault enjoys listening and talking with Raymond Sintès, a pimp who is disliked in the neighborhood. When asked what his profession is, Raymond says that he is a warehouse man. It makes no difference to Meursault that Raymond lies, or that Raymond is a pimp. He likes him; that's reason enough for their casual friendship.

Unlike Meursault, Raymond is a violent person. One can almost see him pacing the room, ready to smash his fist into a wall to release his frustrated anger, while Meursault sits this evening, enjoying some wine, half-listening to Raymond's harangues. Meursault seems to be in the room and, yet, not in the room. He is an observer (remember, for example, how he noted that the sky was "green" on his way home from work, as he also notes the color of the scabs on Salamano's dog), and he is an outsider to Raymond's intensity. Raymond, on the other hand, says that he's merely short-tempered, but admits that he has just fought with a fellow who annoyed him and, while the man was lying on the ground, Raymond continued kicking him: "He was bleeding like a pig when I'd done with him." Besides being somewhat of an outcast in this neighborhood, it would seem that he does not have many friends at all. Thus he comes to Meursault, only a casual friend, for advice and says that if Meursault will help him, he will be Meursault's "friend for life." Meursault's lack of a comment is typical; he has no objection to helping the fellow and has already agreed to eat supper and have some wine with Raymond.

Raymond's desire for revenge against his girlfriend is revealed as soon as supper begins. Like the man whom he continued kicking, even though the man was lying beaten on the ground, Raymond now says that he wants to further punish this girl, whom he has beaten on occasion until "the blood came," but, he adds, he beat her "only affectionately-like."

To say that Raymond is violent is an understatement; he is a sadist. Because the girl slept with someone else, he wants to turn her in to the police as a common prostitute, and he has also considered branding her. Once more, Meursault offers no opinion as to a course of action. What is Meursault's opinion? In his own words, "I said I hadn't any," continuing, however, that he finds the story interesting.

Meursault does not judge; he has no strongly positive or negative reactions to the girl's plight. One can never be sure what to do—this is Meursault's comment, as he drinks more wine. And, with more wine shared between the two men, Meursault agrees to write a scathing letter, making the girl repent of her unfaithfulness; then if she does, Raymond will spit in her face and throw her out of the room. Meursault agrees that such a plan would punish her, but he writes the letter mainly to satisfy Raymond. Why not? Meursault has no reason not to satisfy Raymond because Meursault doesn't really care one way or the other.

For Meursault, what he has done is merely a gesture; it takes no trouble to write such a letter and, besides, Raymond has been generous with his wine and food and cigarettes. Thus we view two very different men as the chapter closes: one is full of fury and revenge; the other has just composed a "real stinker" of a letter, with no personal malice.

At this point, one might ask himself why Meursault writes a letter discrediting the girl. Raymond, we must remember, is not a close friend; the letter is an attempt at deep revenge. This act is unlike Meursault, for usually he is a truthful man, yet here he fabricates a letter to be used for one purpose: to humiliate a girl. Meursault is not, we realize, a thoroughly honest man. His indifference, in this case, is an indifference to truth, for Raymond asks him to write a letter "that'll get her on the raw." Meursault does so, with the help of Raymond's wine; he composes a letter that states not facts, but a letter that will arouse violent emotions. And why? For Meursault, what he has done is a simple act, seemingly, of no great importance; for Raymond, what Meursault has helped him accomplish is monumental. In fact, what Meursault has done, is, indeed, very monumental, for had he not written the letter, he would not have found himself later intertwined in Raymond's problems; he would not have shot an Arab friend of the girl, and he would not have been guillotined.

The chapter ends poetically; whether this is Camus or Meursault commenting, one cannot be certain for Meursault describes the "sleep-bound" house and the moans of Salamano's dog rising slowly "like a flower growing out of the silence and darkness." We have seen rare moments of deeply poetic sensitivity within Meursault, so perhaps Meursault is far more intelligent and sensitive than we have seen until now. Yet this sentence is almost startling, coming from a man who says, in effect, frequently, that most things "don't matter much." If the night moans are compared to fruitful beauty, surely Camus intends irony for this chapter initiates Meursault's doom.

CHAPTER IV

A work week passes and Camus resumes his story on Sunday. It has been a busy week, the letter which Meursault wrote for Raymond has been sent, and Meursault has seen two movies with Emmanuel. Emmanuel doesn't seem too bright because Meursault has to explain what is happening on the screen. Remember, too, that in the last chapter, it was Emmanuel who suggested that he and Meursault try and run fast enough to jump on the fire truck, a rather foolhardy, impulsive act, even if they did it for sheer fun. Meursault, though, doesn't complain that he has to explain to

Emmanuel throughout the movies; likewise, he didn't consider the danger of jumping on a fast-moving fire truck. In both cases, Meursault enjoys himself—the physical exertion of running for the truck and the quiet, monotonous, running analysis of the movies.

Meursault remembers the day before, Saturday, primarily because of Marie's sensuality. Her bright-colored dress, her leather sandals, her breasts, and her tanned face remind him of a "velvety brown flower." Meursault's sensitivity is sensual as he recalls their sucking foam from the sea waves and spouting it toward the sky. This is not the indifferent Meursault of so many situations. This is a man who has an authentic, almost spiritual intimacy with the world. What he describes is a game that he and Marie played, but it was a game of much value for Meursault. Marie and the sea are, in a sense, both sexual partners for him. But, instantly, when the sea becomes too salty, Meursault reacts; he does not enjoy it any longer. And when Marie's kiss is finished, he is ready to swim back to the beach, catch the bus and, at home, make love, feeling the cool air on their sun-brown bodies. Stimulating moments, like these, are rare for Meursault, but they have a richly primitive and personal value for him and enable us to understand this man.

Later, when Marie asks him if he loves her, Meursault answers, honestly, that he supposes that he does not; he says, "that sort of question [has] no meaning, really." The sea, the sun, the waves, kisses, sex—Meursault can touch and feel, but love is too abstract, too ambiguous, and too all-encompassing to ponder. When Marie laughs, Meursault wants to kiss her; that he can understand and delight in. Love, however, is only a word, an over-used word, defined with a sense of permanence. Meursault is permanently bonded to no one—except with moments of spontaneous joy.

Following this scene, centering on love and love-making, Camus juxtaposes a violent battle scene between Raymond and his girlfriend. This becomes a loud battle that quickly gathers a crowd of people. Marie, seeing the woman being knocked about, reacts as most people would. She thinks that this is horrible and that someone should call for a policeman. Quite in character, Meursault observes the battle and comments that he isn't going for a policeman; he doesn't like them. Meursault doesn't care if the girl is being beaten up. Furthermore, it was Meursault who wrote the letter that caused this quarrel. The fate of the girl is of no concern to him. What matters to Meursault is that he dislikes policemen. Note also that the girl is an Arab. Meursault and Raymond and Marie are French. The girl is a native, the police are native; why inject oneself, a Frenchman, into a stormy lovers' quarrel with an Arab?

When a policeman does arrive to settle the argument, he makes a telling observation about Raymond. He accuses Raymond of having drunk so much that Raymond cannot stand steady. Raymond admits that he is trembling, but denies that he has been drinking. His rage has so infuriated him that he has become like a madman. He is, in fact, a man of uncontrollable urges and temper.

There is also a short, revealing scene following the battle. Marie is so upset that she has no appetite for eating her lunch; Meursault eats nearly all of his lunch. Earlier, when Raymond explained to the policeman that his trembling was "only natural," we realized that it indeed was. Now, Meursault's appetite, after just witnessing the end of a fight has not changed and this does not bother him, nor is he bothered that Marie has no appetite. Meursault would say of his actions and attitude exactly what Raymond told the policeman, "That's only natural."

Still later, when Raymond is discussing the fight and Raymond questions Meursault as to whether Raymond should have hit the policeman for knocking a cigarette out of Raymond's mouth, Meursault can only verbally shrug: "I told him I hadn't expected anything whatsoever and, anyhow, I had no use for the police." This is a typical reply for Meursault. His lack of interest, however, does not disturb Raymond, who suggests their taking a stroll, then confesses that he wants Meursault to act as his witness.

Meursault's answer is exactly the same as when Raymond asked if the two men could be friends: "I had no objection." Meursault didn't know what to expect the policeman to do and he doesn't know what Raymond expects him to say. He is not a "programmed" individual, in the social sense. He does not envision or consider the varying consequences of a given situation.

Raymond's pleasure at Meursault's reply is evident. He has a witness for himself; he punished his girlfriend and feels absolutely justified and Meursault will bear witness that the girl provoked and deserved the beating. Raymond is even happier later in the evening when he wins a game of billiards with Meursault. And he laughs when Salamano tells them that he has lost his dog at the fair and that he, Salamano, will *not* pay for a dog he hates — even if the dog dies at the dog pound.

Later, while Salamano paces his room, wheezing, even weeping, there appears a crack in the often abstracted neutrality of Meursault's character. He thinks of his mother and he has no appetite and goes to bed without supper. This is all we know. He tells us no more. Like the staccato-worded telegram which Meursault received at the beginning of the novel, we feel a sense of loss at not knowing more. But Camus' novel is not a journal of Meursault's feelings; it is not an illuminating confession; instead, it is often more like an album of black-and-white snapshots.

CHAPTER V

After a Sunday that was more unusual than most of his Sundays, Meursault begins another week of work, another week of monotony, doing the robot-like actions that most people perform in order to make a living, the same monotony that Camus despises because of its intoxicating, suffocating effect on the human soul. Meursault, as we see from the beginning of this chapter, is what one might call a "good employee." He is annoyed that Raymond telephones him about a personal matter; this is not done. Such telephoning is frowned on by Meursault's superior and Meursault wants to have no trouble with him. He is not free, as he was at the beach, as he was when he ran to catch the fire truck, or when he leaves work and leisurely strolls home. Meursault's work may be dull, but it must be done, and he becomes, at the office, uneasy that he is violating office rules and wasting time. At home, he would not give the idea of chatting on the phone, or of wasting time, a second thought, but his freedom is restricted here.

Raymond's call has two purposes; first, he invites Meursault to spend next Sunday at the seaside with a friend; and, naturally, Meursault, as we have seen, is delighted at the prospect of swimming and sunning and also happy when he learns that he can bring Marie with him. Raymond's second reason for calling is typical of something Raymond might do; he thinks that he is being followed by some Arabs. Raymond, as we have seen, is highly emotional and would be fascinated by the thought of a threat to him by some Arabs. One of them, he tells Meursault, is surely the brother of the girl whom he beat up.

At this point, Meursault is summoned to his employer's office and he becomes queasy, sure that he is to be reprimanded for his personal telephone conversations. Meursault, for the present, is not the unemotional and indifferent Meursault whom we have seen so frequently. He wants no trouble at work. But he quickly metamorphoses into the familiar Meursault when he is told that his company is opening a branch office in Paris and that Meursault has been selected, if he chooses, to work in the Paris office. Most people would be ecstatic, if offered the opportunity to move from Algiers to Paris, but Meursault's reply to his superior is that he is "prepared to go." To us, Meursault seems to be saying that he doesn't care much one way or the other. We puzzle at his reaction — until we read farther and discover what Meursault was really thinking during his conversation with his superior.

Thus, already this morning, Meursault has two promises — one that includes good friends and swimming, and the other, a move to Paris. Most people associate Paris with romance, love, music, gaiety, and reveries. Not Meursault. He reacted to his superior as if his present life suited him and that one life is as good as another. Paris or Algiers — it would, seemingly, make no difference where Meursault worked and lived. It is probably true that he has no intense ambition to receive new promotions and amass a fortune by working his way up through the business ranks of his firm, but we do know that Paris is antithetical to everything we know about Meursault. The city would be repugnant to him; it is bleak, rainy, the sun is rare, and warmth and swimming are very important to Meursault's moments of happiness.

For the first time, we have a small nugget of Meursault's past slipped to us. He remembers once that he did have ambition, but that when he had to drop his studies, he gave up and decided that all of his ambitions were futile. Seemingly, from that time on, he has been the come-what-may, indifferent Meursault.

This nonchalance is emphasized even further when Marie asks Meursault to marry her. He says that he doesn't mind; if she wants to get married, he will marry her "if it will give her pleasure." This attitude is almost identical to Raymond's proposal that he and Meursault become friends. At that time, Meursault replied that he "had no objections."

Meursault's honesty is disarming, for whereas he did not mind one way or the other about writing a letter for Raymond that would punish a girl, fattening the letter, in all probability, with insinuations and, perhaps, even lies, Meursault cannot lie about his own feelings.

He cannot please Marie by saying that he loves her; he will marry her, perform this physical and legal act, but he cannot lie and say that he loves her. Marriage, to him, is of no great importance, just as the exact day on which his mother died is of no great importance. Meursault is an unusually taciturn man. Raymond offered friendship; Marie herself, and now Meursault is offered a new position in Paris. And it all makes no difference, he says; he doesn't object.

Meursault's attitude confuses Marie and it seems a bit unusual to Raymond, but Raymond doesn't mull over the matter as Marie does. Marriage, for her, is a very serious business. She is most ordinary and is described in the most matter-of-fact terms. She likes sex and wants a home and a husband and children. She is unusual only in that she is willing to marry Meursault even after he admits that he would marry any girl that he had been sleeping with and who proposed to him. She rationalizes that perhaps it's Meursault's strangeness that fascinates her, but she is not truly satisfied with the explanation. She threatens Meursault that she may hate him one day, but even that taunt has no emotional thrust, for Meursault says nothing, for a while, until he tells her of the move to Paris, which he describes as dingy, full of masses of pigeons and dark courtyards and pasty-faced people.

Marriage and Paris! Marie's evening is complete. She has her ambitions fulfilled. But she cannot dine with Meursault and wonders why he doesn't ask her why, implying that she might have a date with another man. Meursault merely looks embarrassed and admits to us that he *did* want to know. It is one of the few times that we see him being dishonest.

Camus finishes the chapter with two episodes — one, involving a woman who eats at Meursault's table in Céleste's restaurant and, afterward, Meursault's conversation with Salamano about the lost dog. Camus gives a great deal of attention to this woman and to Meursault's observation of her. Meursault is curious, fascinated by the woman. She is robot-like, moving jerkily, raptly attentive, adding up the bill in advance, wolfing down her food voraciously and checking off from a radio magazine which programs she intends to listen to (which seem, to Meursault, to be practically every one). Robot-like, in fact, is the word which Meursault uses to describe her exit from the cafe. On the surface, this is an incident with no meaning, a strange person who shares his table and whom he watches and someone whom he says he will soon forget about.

Later, in Part Two of the novel, she will be watching Meursault himself as he stands trial for the murder of an Arab.

The love-hate relationship between Salamano and his dog is an illustration of how very different, emotionally, old Salamano is from Meursault. Because Meursault has nothing to do, he listens to the old man's tale. In fact, Meursault offers to the grieving old man a gesture of a so-called white lie: he tells Salamano that his dog looked "well bred." This is not how Meursault described the dog heretofore. Salamano's grief over the dog is a contrast to Meursault's lack of grief over his mother's dying and, in both cases, there are uncertainties. Salamano does not know if his dog is dead, found and housed by someone else, or merely lost; Meursault isn't sure when his mother died. But he listens to Salamano, not because he was concerned about the dog but because, he says, he wasn't sleepy anyway.

Salamano acquired the dog after his wife died; he didn't get along well with her either. To Salamano, who fed the dog, at first from a bottle, the dog was like a child or a baby, but because a dog's life is short and the man was getting old, they both became very old at the same time. Once, he had taken pride in the dog's appearance (and probably in his own), then the dog developed skin trouble that was incurable. When Salamano leaves, Meursault tells us that he "could feel the scales on his skin." The old man hopes that the dogs won't bark in the night, for he always thinks of the dog barking as possibly being his. He wants no false hopes, no false promises that the dog will return. This time the chapter ends on a sad note of resignation, rather than earlier, when the dog's moan was described as being like "a flower growing out of the silence and the darkness."

Perhaps one of the most important, but small bits of information that we receive in this chapter is Salamano's off-hand comment that some of the people in the neighborhood have begun to say nasty things about Meursault, now that his mother is dead. Meursault is not an invisible man anymore. He is already marked as someone who cared so little for his mother that he sent her away. Salamano's affirmation of his friendship and his saying that he knows that Meursault was devoted to his mother is of little comfort to Meursault. The man is clearly disturbed. He tries to explain that he could not afford to keep her any longer and that, for years, they hadn't spoken to one another and that at the Home, he hoped that perhaps she could make friends. Here, in a capsule form is an important part of Meursault's defense in Part Two. Salamano only half-listens to Meursault; he has his own troubles. It will not be an easy night for either man.

CHAPTER VI

Sundays, for Meursault, are usually stagnant days – no routine, no fun, no impromptu outings. This Sunday, however, is the climax of the novel's action, leading us to Meursault's philosophical insight and conversion and, then, to his decapitation. Other than Meursault's mother's funeral, which was described somewhat journalistically, nothing much has happened in the novel until now; thus, Meursault's opening comment in this chapter, describing what an effort it was to get up this morning is ironically comical, reminding one, if he knows anything at all about this novel, of the old saying, "It was one of those mornings when I should have stayed in bed." Certainly this is true in Meursault's case. Marie has to shout at him to rouse him, and as they want to get to the beach early, they don't bother to prepare any breakfast, which is of little concern to Meursault: he has a headache, his first cigarette tastes bitter, and he feels limp and drained. Marie comments that he looks "like a mourner at a funeral," a remark that is part of Camus' irony. During his mother's wake and funeral, Meursault looked the least like a mourner of all those who came to the long vigil around his mother's coffin. If, in fact, someone mistakenly believed that Meursault's behavior was that of a mourner, he was mistaken; Meursault, during those long hours, was not in mourning; he was uncomfortable and embarrassed. He was mourning only in the sense that he was wasting the day and that he had to endure the lengthy and boring ordeal.

Marie's mood this Sunday morning is in direct contrast with Meursault's; she is happy and laughing; Meursault comments that she looked quite ravishing.

This day, as we will discover, is Meursault's last day of physical freedom, his last day to enjoy swimming and sunning and being with Marie, and Camus has already prepared us for this most unusual and fateful day by blackening Meursault's waking mood and accentuating it with the brightness of Marie's gaiety.

After knocking on Raymond's door, letting him know that they are ready to leave, Meursault and Marie go on down the street, but, again, Camus has Meursault remind us that he feels "rather under the weather." It is important that this chapter is studied carefully, for its climax, Meursault's murder of the Arab, should contain a motive for killing the Arab, a key issue. It is extraordinary that Meursault feels particularly bad, most unusual for someone who was eagerly anticipating this bit of a holiday. This day was looked forward to, providing Meursault a chance to get away to the beach and do some swimming and sunning with Marie.

Moments later, Meursault describes himself as not only feeling rather ill, physically, but as if he were struck down, smashed by the glare of the morning sun. Camus is presenting us here with more irony, for if there is anything that Meursault loves, it is the sun. The sun, indeed, has already become almost a character in this novel; we have seen Meursault's delight in its warmth. Today, however, it is too strong and too powerful for him. It hits him in the eyes "like a clenched fist." Once again, Camus stresses and accents Meursault's condition by repeating Marie's reactions to the Sunday morning. To her, the day is glorious. She keeps repeating, "What a heavenly day!" Heavenly is the antithesis of hellish, and hellish the day will certainly become prior to the murder. There is a constant negative-positive counterpoint in this chapter as it builds slowly and tensely towards its climax.

Like Marie, Raymond is in high spirits, addressing Marie in mock graciousness as "Mademoiselle"; he is wearing sports clothes that Meursault finds unattractive and is also wearing a straw hat that makes Marie giggle. In addition, he is wearing a short-sleeved shirt that exposes his rather hairy, white forearms. Meursault is truly in a bad mood to make note of such inconsequential matters.

After commenting on Raymond's outing clothes, Meursault partially explains his feeling of depression. He tells us that the previous evening he had gone to the police station and had testified that Raymond's explanation about beating the Arab girl because of her infidelity was true. The police chose to believe Meursault and, as a result, they released Raymond with merely a warning. Meursault says, "They didn't check my statement." He is saying, in effect, that he lied. Meursault does not know if the girl was actually unfaithful to Raymond; he is indifferent to whether or not she had sex with someone else. He simply had no objection to writing a "real stinker" of a letter for Raymond and testifying that Raymond's reason for the brawl was due to infidelity. Meursault, Camus is stressing, has lied and this is unusual for a man who refuses to lie about his own feelings and actions. He, therefore, is not the one-dimensional victim of this novel, as he is sometimes characterized, nor is he a martyr who has done no wrong (other than shedding no tears at his mother's funeral) and yet is guillotined.

The action quickens even before the trio board the bus, for Raymond points out to Meursault that some Arabs are watching them. Meursault sees them and says that the Arabs looked at them as though they were blocks of stone or dead trees. Raymond even knows which Arab is the brother of the girl whom he abused. Raymond's moods fluctuate, at this point. He is, at least to Meursault, seemingly worried, yet he laughs and says that the brawl is "ancient history," but halfway to the bus stop, he glances back for reassurance that the Arabs are not following them. He does this as a man, fearful of death, might look toward the sky for buzzards circling overhead.

On the bus, Raymond's nervousness becomes flirtatious; he "kept making jokes," Meursault says, in order to amuse Marie, although she seemed unaware of him, nodding at Meursault every now and then and smiling at him. There is a tenseness at this point; we wait for something to happen as they journey toward the beach, the scene of the murder.

The three have left the city and are alone as they walk toward the beach; they are far removed from even the Sunday business of Algiers. Wild lilies are snow-white against the sky, which Meursault describes as being so blue that it has a "metallic glint." During Meursault's silent observations, Marie, child-like, amuses herself by swishing her bag against the flowers and showering their petals. The landscape is described here in portent fragments. As Marie innocently destroys the flowers, Meursault notes that some of the houses are "half-hidden," and that others are "naked from the stony plateau." When at last they reach the beach, a big headland juts out over the sea's "black reflection."

After meeting Raymond's friend, Masson, and his wife, Meursault notices Marie chatting with Masson's wife, laughing, and he tells us that, for the first time, he "seriously" considers the possibility of his marrying her. Remember that he promised her that he would marry her earlier. Now, he "considers" the "possibility" of marrying her. Meursault promised that he would marry Marie, meaning that, for him, at that moment, he "had no objection." He is, above all, a man of present moments, and this present revelation, when he tells us of his actually considering marrying Marie is quite important in understanding this enigmatic man.

Meursault is happy, at this present moment, on the beach. He basks in the sunlight and feels better. The sun, in fact, is a restorative to Meursault, as it usually is. We have heard him speak of it often and we have seen how he reacts to it and how he reacts to his memories of Paris and its lack of sun.

Swimming makes Meursault presently feel even better, particularly the physical contact of his body against the cold water beneath him and the hot sun above him, when his arms and shoulders emerge. There is much emphasis here on this series of present moments, as Meursault and Marie swim, side by side, in rhythm, matching their movements, enjoying, as Meursault says, "every moment."

Meursault eventually becomes so completely relaxed that, after swimming back to the beach and drying in the warmth of the sun and Marie's body, he naps for a short time. Then he rouses at Marie's insistence and the two swim awhile longer, twining around one another. Meursault is so physically satisfied that his senses tingle. He is "ravenously" hungry for lunch and eats much bread and fish and steak and potato chips. Masson, the host, enjoys Raymond's friend and is quick to refill Meursault's wine glass whenever it is empty.

By the time that coffee is being poured, Meursault describes himself as feeling "slightly muzzy," and he starts smoking one cigarette after another. The two couples and Raymond feel deep, empathetic rapport as they discuss spending the entire month of August on the beach together, sharing expenses.

One might think that after Meursault and his friends have spent time on the bus to the beach, swimming, napping, lunching, and discussing plans to summer in the bungalow during August, that it must be mid-afternoon by now. It is not: Marie announces that it is only half-past eleven, which causes her to laugh again. And it is then that Masson proposes that the men take a stroll on the beach while the women clean up the luncheon dishes.

Leaving the house, Meursault first notices the sun, just as he first noticed it when he emerged from his apartment house in Algiers. This time, however, he describes it not as a fist smashing against him, but he comments on its glare; this, combined with the reflection from the water sears his eyes, he says. By now, high noon is approaching, and Meursault sees shimmers of heat rising from the rocks, the beach deserted, and he tells us that one can hardly breathe.

While his attention is paralyzed by the heat of the sun, the glare from the sea, and the intoxicating effect of the wine, Raymond and Masson talk together, Meursault sensing that the two men have known each other for a long time. They walk by the water's edge and, one more time, Meursault mentions the heat and glare on the sea as the sun "beats down" on his bare head. The effect is numbing. Meursault feels half-asleep.

A moment later, he notices two Arabs coming toward them from a long way down the beach. Raymond is immediately apprehensive, as is his nature, sure that one of the Arabs is his girl friend's brother. Meursault says nothing, as is his usual nature. Raymond is ready for a scuffle, planning to fight one Arab himself and the hefty Masson taking the other. Meursault is to stand by to help if another Arab appears. The sun broils on the two clusters of men approaching one another along the edge of the sea. And, besides the sun blazing from above them, below them the sand is "as hot as fire." Meursault swears that it is "glowing red."

The confrontation occurs when the men are only a few steps apart. Raymond steps forward and when one of the Arabs lowers his head, Raymond lashes out, shouting at Masson. Masson throws his appointed Arab into the sea, and Raymond, proud of punishing "his" already bleeding Arab, foolishly breaks for a moment to shout to Meursault that he "ain't finished yet," hoping to beat this Arab the same way that he did the Arab's sister. In that moment, the Arab reaches for his knife and slashes Raymond on the arm and on the mouth.

Frightened by Masson's hulking appearance, both Arabs begin to back away slowly, the knife held before them; when they are a distance from the Frenchmen, they begin to run.

Raymond seems to be wounded badly; blood is running from his arm and when he tries to talk, blood bubbles from his mouth. By chance, however, once they are back at the bungalow, they discover that the wounds are not deep and that Raymond will be able to walk to a nearby doctor.

Masson accompanies Raymond and Meursault is left behind with the women; Marie is quite pale and Mme. Masson is crying. Ostensibly, Meursault is left behind to guard the women and also to explain to them what has happened. It is difficult to imagine him as a proficient guard and, as he admits, he doesn't say much about what has happened. He prefers to stare at the sea.

Raymond is unhappy when he returns, even though he has been assured by the doctor that his wounds are not serious and he is emphatic when he says that he is going for a walk on the beach, that he wants to be alone, and that he wants *no one* to accompany him. In fact, he "flies into a rage." Meursault, however, as we have often seen, does as he pleases. He follows Raymond, despite Masson's objections.

It is approaching two o'clock now, and Meursault describes the afternoon as feeling like a furnace, the sunlight splintering into "flakes of fire" on the sand and on the sea. Meursault continues to follow Raymond, and Raymond continues to walk until he finds what he has been seeking—the two Arabs, who seem quite docile now, one staring without speaking, the other playing three notes on a little reed flute. This, then, is Camus' tableau: no one moving and no one speaking. All is hot sunlight and heavy silence, and the reed flute and a tinkling sound from a small stream. The scene seems almost idyllic.

Without warning, Raymond asks Meursault if he should shoot the girl's brother. Meursault explains to us that he says the first thing that comes into his head; this is usually what he has always done. This time, though, his answer is tempered, for he knows that Raymond's ire might well be responsible for a murder. Meursault says it would be a "low-down trick" to shoot the Arab "in cold blood." Raymond is not to be so easily persuaded; he will say something sufficiently provocative that he will have a chance to gain revenge on the man who has maimed him. This was his same tactic with the girl; he wrote a note which so provoked her that he was able to further punish her.

Again, Meursault warns Raymond that he should not fire unless the Arab draws his knife, but Raymond is beginning to fidget. Both of the Arabs watch them like cautious, alert animals, revealing no emotion or movement, yet watching Raymond and Meursault all the time and observing Raymond's building excitement and Meursault's hesistancy. When Meursault asks for the gun, we instinctively feel that if Meursault has the gun, he will not use it. We are certain that Raymond needs little reason for using it.

The sun glints on the revolver. Again, as though it is a character in this drama of death, the sun asserts itself. Then all is silence and during the silence, Meursault comes to the conclusion that "one might fire, or not fire—" and it "would come to absolutely the same thing." Recall that when he was offered a position in the Paris office, his thoughts were similar: he "didn't care much one way or the other." When the subject of a "change of life" was introduced by his employer, he answered that "one life was as good as another," and that his present life suited him quite well. Later, when Marie asked him to marry her, he said he "didn't mind; if she was keen on it, [they would] get married." Meursault has been mesmerized by the heat into his former, almost total, indifference to matters at hand. Here he stands with a gun, able to kill another man and he thinks, "it would come to absolutely the same thing." The situation has no meaning, no importance to him. The Arabs are not really men to Meursault; a death, a marriage, a move to Paris—nothing is of absolute importance to him.

Suddenly the Arabs vanish. So quickly do they accomplish this that it is as though they were like lizards, slipping under the cover of a rock. So, it would seem, ends the stand-off duel, and Raymond and Meursault turn and walk back, Raymond talking about taking the bus back to Algiers.

But while Raymond seems happier, Meursault has changed. The light thuds within his head and he feels that he hasn't the energy to walk up the steps to the bungalow. He stresses continuously that the heat is too great. He cannot move; it is "blinding light falling from the sky. And his leitmotif occurs again: "To stay, or to make a move—it came to much the same." He does not know what to do and it is purely by chance that his decision is not one that he has reasoned. He simply starts walking—returning to the beach. For no reason, with no stated intent, other than a vague recollection of the coolness behind the rock, a retreat from the fiery afternoon, he returns to the beach. As he walks slowly ahead, there is a red glare as far as he can see and he can hear small waves lapping at the hot sand. Meursault's temples are throbbing and he feels that the heat is trying to force him back, pressing on him, trying to check any progress that he might attempt to make. Hot blasts strike at him repeatedly as he grits his teeth and clenches his fist in defiance of a universe that he will not allow domination over him. Camus' description of Meursault's walk toward the beach becomes almost like that of a battle—Meursault pitted against the sun. He clenches his fists, he grits his teeth; blades of light shoot toward him from broken glass and shells. His jaw sets more firmly, more determinedly. We have never seen Meursault so intent, so purposelessly intent on accomplishing nothing other than reaching the cool stream. He is, very simply, defying a force that opposes him.

When he sees a small black hump of rock, he can think only of one thing—the cold, clear stream behind it and his longing to hear the tinkling of running water. His goal is finally definite: to be rid of the sun, the women in tears, and retrieve the cool silence behind the shadow of the rock.

Someone else has done the same thing; the brother of Raymond's girl friend has reclaimed his spot behind the rock. Meursault had completely forgotten about the Arabs. Not once while he was staggering toward the rock had he thought about the Arabs; now Raymond's enemy has possessed the cool safety from the sun. Both men react immediately and naturally. Despite Meursault's weariness, one cannot say now that Meursault is totally indifferent to the Arab; this is mutual fear that we view, each of the men simultaneously reaching for their weapons when they encounter one another. Meursault grips Raymond's pistol in the pocket of his coat and the Arab's hand goes to the pocket of his coat, where he keeps his knife. To Meursault, the Arab, even though only ten yards away, is only a blurred, dark form, wobbling in the heat haze. At times, Meursault can see glimpses of the Arab's eyes, glowing against the sound of the waves and the weight of the molten sun.

A sense of the rational returns to Meursault. He has no quarrel with this Arab; their relationship seems an empty, meaningless one. But Meursault *did* write the letter; he has forgotten that fact as he thinks that all he need do is turn his body around, move his feet, and walk away and think no more about the Arab. But he cannot. He feels the sun pulsing within the sand beneath his feet, pressing up the length of his body and, instead of turning, Meursault moves toward the stream and toward the Arab. The heat scorches his cheeks and sweat gathers in his eyebrows; this heat is akin to the smothering heat during his mother's funeral. Then, as now, especially in Meursault's forehead, he feels as though he cannot bear for another instant the heaviness of the sun; a moment more and his veins will burst through the skin. He takes a step forward and, at that moment, the Arab draws his knife, holding it up, causing the sun to travel the length of the blade and "pierce" Meursault's forehead, transfixing him. Sweat splashes down his eyelids, veiling his eyes with salty brine. Meursault is conscious of nothing except the sun on his skull and the blade of knife-light, "slicing" into his eyeballs.

He begins to reel as he describes the fiery gust that comes from the sea, the sky cracking in two and a great sheet of flame "pouring down." Meursault tells us that at that moment "the trigger gave, and the smooth underbelly of the butt jogged my palm." Reality, at this point, has vanished for Meursault. There is no conscious gripping the trigger, aiming and firing; the trigger "gave way" and, as it were, the gun fired and Meursault heard a "crisp, whipcrack sound." He does not tell us that he saw the Arab's body fall; he does not tell us much more at all, only that he fired four more shots into the dead body and yet could see no visible trace of the bullets entering the body. We have witnessed a murder. There is a dead body which Meursault continues to fire into, yet there seems to be no evidence of a murder, no visible signs of a murder.

The chapter ends with the emphasis not so much on the murder of the Arab, but on Meursault's return to consciousness. He is aware that he has committed an act that is of prime importance. For once in his life, which heretofore had been assembled of meaningless acts, he has acted so definitely that the consequences will not be meaningless, will matter one way or another. He knows, he says, that he has destroyed the "balance of the day." Until Meursault composed the letter for Raymond, he simply lived; nothing very exciting ever happened to him; days began and days ended and these days added up into monotonous years. This was not so following the letter and the beating of the Arab girl. The Arabs have a natural resentment for their French colonial invaders and a human desire for revenge. Meursault, by chance, by "having no objection," became involved in Raymond's emotional escapades and, by chance, Meursault murders the man who once stalked Raymond.

Meursault is jolted, knowing that he has desecrated the calm of the beach on which he had been so happy. It is then that he fires four more shots into the dead Arab, knowing that each successive shot is undoing a life of rhythmic drifting. He is creating for himself his own "undoing," as he puts it. The cymbals of the sun clashing inside his head have climaxed a former life which drifted toward an uncertain death. Now he faces a life directed toward a certain death.

PART TWO

CHAPTER I

The first chapter of Part Two is narrated in Meursault's frequent matter-of-fact tone, describing his first interrogation by police officials. At first, he says, nobody seemed to have much interest in his case. Interestingly, this attitude is, more or less, how Meursault views the matter. He is not deeply concerned about his case or the possibility that he has committed the ultimate of crimes — murder. Instead of his telling us about his internal feelings, which he seems to ignore or lack, he describes, in bare outlines, the boredom of the police official's questioning and the repetition of giving again and again his name and address and occupation. Meursault has so little comprehension of what is happening that he is surprised when an examining magistrate asks him if he has obtained a lawyer. Meursault's answer is succinct and honest: no, of course not. To Meursault, it didn't seem necessary to find a lawyer, consult with the lawyer, and pay this man a large fee for defending him. That would be too much trouble and Meursault is not sure that it is necessary for him even to have a lawyer. He is, in fact, pleased to learn that the court will appoint a lawyer for the defense; all the bothersome details will be taken care of. To him, this is "an excellent arrangement"; he won't have to waste his time with petty trivials.

Whereas Meursault's first examination took place at the police station and was uneventful, the examination, a week later, before a magistrate is different. To the earlier police officers who questioned Meursault, he was faceless; he was simply a Frenchman who had shot an Arab. This new magistrate, however, eyes Meursault with distinct curiosity. This magistrate recognizes that Meursault is not a typical murderer. From the first, he is curious and even amused at Meursault's naivete when he is queried about a lawyer. Meursault blandly answers again that he hadn't thought about obtaining the services of a lawyer. Meursault still does not know whether or not a lawyer is necessary, for a lawyer still seems superfluous; we know Meursault killed an Arab and he knows that he killed an Arab. He is confronted with legal mechanics and is a stranger in this new world, without any knowledge of this foreign, legalistic environment.

Whereas his former life had been lived in fragments, this new life is a highly regimented system.

To Meursault, his case is simple. Lawyers are only necessary when a case contains a multiplicity of details, ambiguities, and there is a reasonable doubt as to the seriousness of the crime. There is nothing to argue about when Meursault's case is on the docket; he is not callous or being canny in displaying such an attitude. It is only a formality that he be required to have a lawyer and he is again relieved to hear that he will not have to bother with certain prescribed formalities.

There is a sense of the examination being surreal to Meursault. He finds himself concentrating on the room where he is being questioned. It is more like a living room than a questioning room for murderers. There is an absurdness about the bourgeois curtains, the dumpy armchair and the simple lamp. Once more, Meursault seems to have removed himself from the scene and seems to be viewing it from another point of view, watching another man answer questions in this "ordinary sitting room." He admits that he doesn't listen to the magistrate very seriously because he has read descriptions of how such examinations are held and this does not conform to the stark, brutal descriptions in novels. This examination, to Meursault, seems "like a game." This is a telling statement. In a preface to the British edition of this novel, Camus states that Meursault is condemned and guillotined because "he doesn't play the game." Meursault dies because he refuses to lie in a court of law; he dies, says Camus in the same preface, "for the sake of truth."

There are no anguished feelings of guilt within Meursault as he relates the details of his interview; instead, he tells us about the physical features of the magistrate, who gives the impression of being highly intelligent except for one small aspect—his mouth has a rather ugly, nervous tic. Camus combines this stroke of description with the ridiculousness of an examination for murder taking place in a living room, suggesting further absurdness when Meursault admits that, when leaving, he does so almost as if he had finished a chat. He is ready to extend his hand and say good-by to the magistrate. Then, momentarily, Meursault remembers that he has killed a man. Yet his use of the word "man" is not wholly convincing. If he felt that he had actually murdered another human being, surely there would be more internal struggling within himself as to why he did it. There seems to be none. And his admission that he remembered "just in time" about the murder is almost an aside, as though he had forgotten something far less important than taking the life of another man.

When Meursault talks with the lawyer that the court has appointed, he agrees to follow the lawyer's advice. The lawyer already knows that Meursault's case is not the simple case that Meursault is convinced it is. For example, he does not like the possibility that he will have to explain Meursault's attitude toward his mother's death. He tells Meursault that the police know that, according to rumors, Meursault showed "great callousness" during his mother's funeral. This matter of Meursault's callousness bothers the lawyer. If Meursault evidenced a lack of feeling during his own mother's funeral, what defense can the lawyer use when he must explain the actions of his client who has murdered a stranger, without motive? He tries to make certain that Meursault realize the seriousness of this charge of callousness. Only Meursault can help himself in this court of law, he says.

Asking Meursault if he felt any grief at all during the funeral, the lawyer is distraught when Meursault replies that the question is terribly odd. Meursault would have been embarrassed to ask anyone such a personal question. He admits that he doesn't think much about his feelings and that his "detachment" has increased in recent years. Most questions are difficult for Meursault to answer, as we have seen, unless he can answer them with a simple yes or no. When a question requires thinking and considering, Meursault becomes confused and wonders why he is being asked such a question, particularly questions with philosophical dimensions. Truthfully, he knows that he was quite fond of his mother. But note that he does not say that he loved her. At this point, Meursault says only that he was "quite fond" of his mother. This is the most positive statement he can make, which does not carry much legalistic clout, especially when one is considering a charge of callous, cold-blooded murder.

Meursault considers himself just a normal man, yet note that the magistrate looks at Meursault with much curiosity and even Marie earlier wondered if Meursault's oddness was one of the reasons she had fallen in love with him. All of the accumulated evidence convinces us that Camus is showing us that Meursault is certainly not "just a normal man." In another example, Meursault reveals something to his lawyer that an ordinary man, in a cell waiting for a trial, would not utter. Meursault says that *all* normal people probably have, at one time or another, wished the death of those they loved. He adds that his thought occurred to him as sort of an after-thought; he does not realize the potential gravity of what he has said. To him, it is just an after-thought, a harmless musing.

It is little wonder that Meursault's lawyer is greatly perturbed. He begs Meursault not to make such damning statements during the trial. And Meursault promises — for one reason: "to satisfy him." He has done this repeatedly; he helped Raymond because he wanted to satisfy him; he promised to marry Marie to satisfy her. But now he warns the lawyer that his promises are not iron-bound. He explains that his "physical condition at any given moment" usually influences what he says and does and how he feels. This is rare insight for Meursault to realize about himself and it is rarer still for him to admit such a statement, when his life depends on convincing a jury that he should not be executed for murdering another man.

With almost child-like innocence, Meursault tells the lawyer that he'd rather that his mother had *not* died. Meursault considers this a strongly positive statement. Merely because he did not weep carries no importance because he was hot and tired that day; were it up to him, his mother would be alive today. But she died. It was not his fault and it is astonishing that the lawyer can place so much importance on the fact that, because of the heat and Meursault's fatigue, that he did not weep at the funeral.

The lawyer, who is what most readers would probably consider "normal," feels sure that Meursault will want to say that on the day of the funeral that he managed to keep his feelings "under control." This is impossible for Meursault to do. It would be a lie. We are not surprised when Meursault says that the lawyer looked at him queerly and seemed slightly revolted, saying that the head of the Home and some of the staff would be witnesses, proving that Meursault was devoid of feelings for his mother. The prosecution has powerful weapons to use against Meursault.

It is beyond Meursault's comprehension what the death of his mother and the death of the Arab have in common. To him, they are two totally unrelated events. The lawyer, however, knows how facts can be twisted and misinterpreted; in this particular case, the prosecution wouldn't even have to make sly, subtle charges. Meursault's attitude toward his mother's death can be used with blatant reminders in order to convince the jury that, before them, is a man who has no feelings, evidenced by witnesses, for his own mother's death. Thus he is capable of killing—because of his lack of feeling. The lawyer warns Meursault that it is evident that the prisoner has never had any dealing with the law. Meursault notes that the lawyer looked "vexed" when he left.

Meursault does not want understanding and sympathy from the lawyer and he admits being tempted, at times, to assure the lawyer that he is only "an ordinary person." But he does not because, as he says, he is too lazy to do so.

Later that day, when Meursault is taken to the examining magistrate's office, he notes, first of all, the intense heat in the room and that it seems to be flooded with light. Already we have seen how sensitive Meursault is to heat and light and so this visit begins badly. The heaviness of the heat is an omen, presaging the magistrate's statement that the lawyer cannot be present and that Meursault may, if he wishes, reserve answering any questions. There is little doubt as to what Meursault will do; he will answer for himself. From the beginning, he saw little use for a lawyer, other than the fact that the Code demanded he have one.

The interrogation is brusque. Meursault, the magistrate says, has the reputation of being taciturn and somewhat self-centered. These charges are negative; one might use other words and say that Meursault is a man who minds his own business and gives nobody any trouble. Meursault's answer to the magistrate's question as to whether or not the charges are true is, one might say, taciturn. Meursault rarely has much to say, so naturally he doesn't say much. He is very logical and very honest as he answers the magistrate. Again, the naivete of Meursault amuses the magistrate, who smiles at the answer, adding that his question, at any rate, has little or no importance, which is exactly what Meursault has said—why say— or ask—anything when there is nothing of importance to be said?

Meursault's uniqueness intrigues the magistrate, who, Meursault notes, leans forward, fastening his eyes deeply and raising his voice a little. The magistrate, obviously, has never interrogated a man who was so bluntly honest. Or perhaps stupid. He admits the charge of murder doesn't interest him as much as Meursault, himself, does. He is puzzled about Meursault's participation in the crime more than he is in the crime itself. Meursault is not puzzled; he assures the magistrate that what happened is quite simple and he is puzzled only that the magistrate wants to hear the story again, for he says that he has told the magistrate about Raymond, the beach, the swimming—all the details—during their first interview. But Meursault consents, rather unwillingly, to retell the story and when he finishes, it is with a sense that he has wasted time repeating what he already has said and that he feels as though he has never talked so much in his life.

The magistrate promises to help Meursault, partly because Meursault interests him, but he questions him, as did the lawyer, about Meursault's relationship with his mother. As to his loving his mother, Meursault says that he did, "like everybody else." There is a noise behind him when the clerk pushes the typewriter carriage back and seems to be crossing something out. This is a moment in which Camus foreshadows the irony of Meursault's discussing love "like everybody else" and his eventual fate, which will be determined by the jury's failure to believe that he can love "like everybody else." As a result, because of an error (the murder) and Meursault's failure to weep at the funeral, he will be crossed out, executed, as efficiently as the typist here corrects an error.

The magistrate's next question causes Meursault to pause before he answers. He emphasizes that he did not shoot five consecutive shots. He tells the absolute truth. He fired one shot, killing the Arab, and then, after a short interval, he fired four more shots. And he cannot explain the interval between the first shot and the others, but he re-lives that instant, probably due to the intense heat and light in the magistrate's room. He sees the glow of the beach hovering again before his eyes. He cannot answer the magistrate's question, even after the magistrate waits, fidgets, half-rises, sits down again and asks for an answer. He insists on an answer, but Meursault remains silent.

Meursault's silence transforms the magistrate, whom Meursault once thought looked like a most intelligent man, into a madman. Waving a silver crucifix, he rants that he believes in God Almighty and that even the worst of sinners (presumably, Meursault) can obtain forgiveness. But, first, the magistrate says, there must be repentance and the sinner must become "like a little child." Again we encounter irony, as we have viewed Meursault's child-like behavior and responses to the magistrate. The madness of the magistrate, in turn, transforms Meursault. He becomes alarmed. This supposedly sane judge of men is brandishing a silver crucifix before Meursault's eyes—a weapon very similar to the knife which the

Arab flashed before Meursault and on which the light blazed. Meanwhile the office is becoming more stiflingly hot and big flies are buzzing on Meursault's cheeks. It is a scene of punishment — by the heat, the flies, and by the magistrate. Meursault realizes that such odd behavior is far more typical of a criminal, and Meursault, enduring silently, is the criminal. Furthermore, he becomes truly criminal to the magistrate when he admits to a disbelief in God. In despair, the magistrate says that if he ever doubted that God existed, his life would have no meaning; it is as though he is accusing Meursault of trying to convert him to being a non-believer, asking Meursault if he wishes the magistrate's life to have no meaning. Child-like, Meursault cannot follow the logic of the magistrate; how could his wishes have any effect on the magistrate's faith in God?

Meursault has had enough and is willing to lie in order to escape from this asylum of heat and talk of sin, but, instinctively, he says that he must have shaken his head, meaning No, when the magistrate asked him a final time if he believed in God.

The silence that follows is similar to the silence between the first shot and the following four shots. The magistrate is convinced, he says, that Meursault is the most hard-hearted criminal he has ever known. Everyone else has wept at the magistrate's performance with the crucifix, the symbol of Christ's suffering. As he did not at his mother's funeral, Meursault does not weep now.

The lawyer and, especially, the examining magistrate have struggled to find and give meaning to their lives. Meursault never bothered to consider whether or not his life had "meaning." His attitude is frightening and threatens the philosophy of society: once one is born, life must be lived and suicide is a sin and one's life must be governed by principles and purposes. This kind of reality, however, is not Meursault's and, for that reason, he is accused of lacking "feeling." Meursault has feelings, but his feelings are not coalesced into a systematic, moral unity.

The interview ended, Meursault admits that he does not feel total regret for what he has done; what he feels is "less regret than a kind of vexation." Subsequently, during the many interrogations with the magistrate, the lawyer accompanies Meursault, attempting to have Meursault amplify his previous statements. And, sometimes, Meursault notices, they take very little notice of him. The magistrate seems to have lost interest in this queer, hard-hearted man who denies the existence of God. To them, Meursault becomes a non-person; neither man is hostile toward him. Ironically, Meursault says that he felt that sometimes he was "one of the family."

The interrogations last eleven months and Meursault is transformed into almost enjoying the ordeals. He takes delight in the magistrate's dismissing him and addressing him as "Mr. Antichrist." Any semblance of reality has been reversed within this court of which is supposedly stark reality.

CHAPTER II

Chapter I of Part Two focused on Meursault's changing relationship with the magistrate and with the lawyer and with his own attitude toward himself during the eleven months of the legal conferences. Chapter II takes those same eleven months and reveals what Meursault did when he was not being interrogated. It focuses on his day-to-day living while in prison. In addition, it illuminates various comments made by Meursault in Chapter I. For example, Meursault said that at times, he felt as though he and the examining magistrate were playing games. Here, he says that despite not wanting to talk about some things that happened, he has decided to recount them. The first which he mentions concerns his sense of unreality. During his early days in prison, he could not comprehend that he was actually being held prisoner. He was hardly conscious of what had happened and that prison was the result of an act which he performed. He had a child-like hope that something would happen, something agreeable and surprising.

Now, matters have changed and Meursault can pinpoint when he lost his reluctance to talk about what happened to him in prison. The change occurred when he received a letter from Marie stating that she would not be able to visit him anymore. She had come to see him only once. But because they were not married, she was denied a wife's privilege. It was on that day, Meursault tells us, that he realized that his cell was his "last home," and, as he puts it, "a dead end."

When he was first arrested, he was taken to a large room filled mostly with Arabs — that is, natives. Meursault is a Frenchman, one of the occupiers of the Algerian colony. It is not surprising that the natives are reluctant to say much to him when he tells them that he has killed an Arab. Afterward, he recounts being put in a small cell with a little window, through which he has glimpses of the sea. He is denied all but a single visitation from Marie, and he is teased by glimpses of the sea he loves to swim in, where he can see sunlight playing on the waves. Here, Camus shows us the ever-present dual role of the sun; at times, it is murderous, while at others it is warming and playful.

Meursault describes his new surroundings almost clinically, detailing the flights of steps, the room, the windows, the grilles, the thirty feet of "no man's land" between the prisoners and their visitors. There, he must face Marie and raise his voice in order for her to hear him. This is a vastly different world for Meursault. Formerly, he spoke only rarely; now, he must raise his voice, among the babel of voices of Arab natives. And even here, he cannot escape the torture of the white, glaring sunlight covering the two groups of desperate people, trying to be heard above the other voices, battling for one another's messages under the sunlight that floods the stark room. Meursault admits that, at first, he felt dizzy, for his cell had been very dark and very silent. Then he was thrust into a world of panic, harshly lit, and peopled with murmurs and whispers of Arabs. For some time, he could not say anything of importance. The reality of prison was beginning to tighten. Marie was pressed against bars, looking pretty, and Meursault wanted to tell her so, give her a simple compliment, yet he was too embarrassed to say so, surrounded by the Arabs. Likewise, Marie's questions are commonplace; she wonders if he is all right and if he has everything he wants. Not only are the questions commonplace; they are ridiculous. Yet he answers affirmatively and quickly. The two become even more separated when the Arabs closest to them begin to interrupt them and comment about their own troubles, and Marie shouts that Raymond sends greetings. Meursault's thanks are drowned by the voice of the man next to him. Meursault desires so much to be free now, to be able to embrace Marie, despite this sea of confusion, to feel her body through her thin dress. She assures him that he will be acquitted and that they will go swimming together again, and says that he must not give up hope. But as one reads of the chaotic shouting and of the drone of the Arabs among themselves, we know that Meursault can have little hope. Even the light outside the window seems to become evil, smearing the faces of the people with a coat of yellowish oil. He feels sick, yet he wants to remain and absorb as much as he can of a single moment of Marie's presence. She continues to smile and talk about her work, and all of Meursault's attention is on her and not on what she is saying. Then he is led away, leaving Marie pressed to the rails, trying to smile.

With Marie's first letter comes Meursault's sharp realization that he must, to keep his sanity, stop thinking like a free man. All of his life he has yielded to impulses; we saw this clearly in Part One of the novel. Now he can no longer go down to the beach for a swim in order to feel the cold water against his body after a hot day at the office. This is no game. He is locked within a narrow cell. This phase of being reminded that he is no longer a free man lasts for a few months only, he says. Then another change occurs.

Meursault began having a "prisoner's" thoughts. Being no longer free to do what he wishes to do on impulse, he looks forward to the few things that he is allowed to do. Small ventures, such as a daily walk in the courtyard of the prison or even a visit from his lawyer become of prime importance. His adjustment pleases him, even though it also surprises him. He likens his imprisonment to being held within the trunk of a tree and being able to see only a patch of sky. Even tortured by that, he is sure that he can adjust. He imagines that if such were the case, he would find pleasure in watching for the passing of birds overhead or watching for drifting clouds. Camus' comments in his *Myth of Sisyphus* are pertinent to Meursault's comments here.

Although condemned to rolling an enormous boulder up a hill, only to watch it tumble back down, Sisyphus adjusted. His mind was his own, although his body was forced to repeat again and again, throughout eternity, the same action. Camus says that when one begins to realize a sense of the absurd, he places a great value on "a single impression, like Proust lingering over the scent of a rose." This is step one: valuing the depth of a single sensation, adjusting to the intoxication of a new lucidity. Here, Meursault is newly aware that if it were possible to claim only a scrap of sky for himself, he could be satisfied. He could define that sky and those moments as absolutes and be content with them. Later, Meursault will change because Camus goes one step further: the absurd man will, finally, abandon single moments, single sensations, and limited visions. He will see the need of "accumulating as many as possible." Yet, for the present, Meursault is excited that he can envision being satisfied with a single patch of sky. It would be reason enough for him to rebel and transcend his punishment. Man has always looked to the heavens for help; and Meursault would be sustained by a corner of the sky for it would infuse within him a desire to continue to live. Death is an absolute end and as long as Meursault had his portion of sky (or, as in reality, his sliver of sea), he has hope, a new awareness of life, and the knowledge that he has the strength to struggle against an incomprehensible court and, ultimately, an incomprehensible world.

Meursault also realizes that, simply, matters could be worse. At least, he is not, literally, bound within the trunk of a tree. He does have the freedom of his narrow cell and the anticipation of wondering what kind of odd necktie his lawyer will appear in next, and it is during these thoughts that he remembers the words of his dead mother. She was frequently saying that "in the long run, one gets used to anything." This is Meursault's first thoughts of his mother that have been positive and not associated in some way with her death or her funeral.

Sex — the lack of it — bothers Meursault, but he has memories of the many women he has had sex with and he can fill his small cell with their faces. Although it may seem a torment to realize that he is no longer free to have sex when he pleases, his memories serve to blot out boredom and time.

Meursault also misses smoking. Cigarettes are forbidden and he tells us that that particular deprivation was "what got me down the most," describing tearing off splinters from his plank bed and sucking on them. He describes in detail the physical symptoms of withdrawal, the feeling of faintness and the biliousness that was constantly with him. He cannot understand why he is not allowed to smoke. It is only when he realizes, again, that he is a prisoner that he understands. He is a prisoner and a prisoner is a person who is being punished. His punishment is a denial of women and cigarettes. But Meursault almost smiles as he admits that when this revelation comes to him, he had lost the craving for cigarettes, so the authorities who denied him cigarettes were no longer able to punish him.

He confesses to being not absolutely unhappy. He quickly learns the trick of defeating boredom by exercising his memory, recounting his apartment's bedroom, for instance, and visualizing every single object in every detail — tiny dents in the woodwork, chipped edges, the exact grain and color of the woodwork. All of these things he had never noticed before. They had simply existed, as he had simply existed. He was as unaware of their importance as they were unaware of him.

He discovers that the more he remembers, the more he is able to remember and concludes that even after a single day's experience in the outside world, if a man were imprisoned for the rest of his life, if he could recall, in the minutest detail, everything about that day, he could fill all his time with memory and not be defeated by boredom. This is compensation, he says. It is also more; it is a victory over the system that hopes to stifle hope and humanity. By remembering, Meursault discovers again a world that did not exist when he lived in it. Now it has come alive for him, but this miracle of sorts was only possible because he is not allowed to live in it.

In addition, Meursault sleeps, and sleep can also blot out the monotony of time. Meursault sleeps so well, in fact, that he has only six hours to fill with memories and fantasies.

He then stops telling of how he spent his time during those eleven months and describes an incident when, one day, while he was inspecting his straw mattress, he found a bit of yellowed newspaper stuck on the underside. Part of the paper is missing, but the newspaper contains the story of a crime, committed in a village in Czechoslovakia. The story is a short one, one in fact that Camus later enlarged into a play, *The Misunderstanding*. The play recounts the story of a young man who leaves home, makes a fortune, and after twenty-five years, returns, hoping to surprise his mother and sister. The two women manage an inn and murder their guest during the night for his money. When the dead man's wife explains what has happened, the mother hangs herself and the sister throws herself into a well. The story intrigues Meursault; he says that he read and re-read the story thousands of times, determining finally that perhaps one shouldn't play tricks of that sort. Perhaps one, indeed, should not play tricks, even tricks that include writing vicious letters that lead to brawls and, in Meursault's case, a murder.

The Misunderstanding was first produced in 1944, several years following the publication of *The Stranger*. Obviously, Camus was very much intrigued with the irony of a mother and a daughter murdering a rich stranger, who, by chance, is their son and brother. The women, it is assumed, have probably murdered other rich strangers who have come to their inn; this particular guest, being alone in the inn, is an easy victim. Thus, as readers, we are confronted with another murder — a murder of, presumably, a stranger.

Unlike Meursault, however, the mother and daughter kill themselves in fits of madness and guilt when they discover the identity of the dead man, whereas, in contrast, Meursault does not fully comprehend his own murder of a stranger.

Camus also teases us with yet another murder and with the philosophical question as to whether or not it makes any difference whether one kills a stranger or, in this case, a son and a brother. Even the title of Camus' play, based on this short tale is ironic. Murder, can under no circumstance, ever be excused as the result of a mere misunderstanding. In the next chapter, Meursault's old friend Céleste will defend Meursault by saying that the murder of the Arab was just an accident, a stroke of bad luck. Likewise, Raymond will defend Meursault by stating that "chance" and "mere coincidence" are to blame. Such statements are true, but are they reason enough to excuse a man for taking another man's life and then firing four additional bullets into the dead corpse? And, in turn, we must ask ourselves if the murderer must pay with his life and be murdered for "the good of society" by the state.

From a former existence of living only for present moments, as a prisoner Meursault is able to comprehend only yesterday and tomorrow with meaning. When the jailer informs him that he has been six months in jail, the words have no meaning; they convey nothing to him. He studies his face in his little tin pannikin to see if he has changed, holding it at various angles, but his face always has the same mournful, tense expression. Watching the sun setting, he hears his voice and realizes that lately he has been talking to himself; he has been unaware that this has been happening. A free man cannot, Meursault says, imagine what evenings are like in prison.

In this new world, where freedom does not exist, time becomes of prime importance for Meursault because it seems endless. The uniformity is unrelieved until Meursault discovers that he can challenge his punishment with memory, with sleep, and the intriguing re-creation in his mind of the account of the murder in the scrap of newspaper clipping. Thus he "murders" time in order to retain a semi-sense of life. *Inside* the walls of his cell, Meursault is, literally, an *outsider*, a stranger to society (*The Outsider*, interestingly, is the British title of this novel). Yet, it is only within his cell that Meursault learns for the first time to fathom that life is valuable and that it can have quality.

CHAPTER III

Because of Meursault's ability to cope with the usual boredom that accompanies imprisonment, he tells us early in this chapter that, in truth, the eleven months he spent in his cell did not pass slowly. He adds that as his trial approaches, another summer has come. Almost a year has passed since he shot the Arab.

On the day Meursault's trial begins, Camus colors it, characteristically, with "brilliant sunshine." Sunshine has been described, metaphorically, in many various guises throughout the novel but, on this particular day, it is "brilliant." There seems to be added hope in the remark of Meursault's lawyer, during which he assures Meursault that the trial will be brief, lasting only two or three days. Meursault's case, it seems, is not important because the case immediately following his deals with the murder of a father by his own son, a trial which probably will take some time.

Meursault is almost relaxed; the sense of game-playing returns as he describes the noises of the courtroom, reminding him of small-town "socials," when a room is being cleared, after a concert, for dancing. He even refuses an offered cigarette, once his greatest deprivation and, further, he anticipates the prospect of witnessing a trial. His own trial does not seem to trouble him at all; he is far more interested in the spectacle of being a witness to another device of the legal machinery that has attempted to control his world for these eleven months. This is a novelty to a man who has had—except in a single instance—no visitors, other than legal interrogators, for almost a year, living in a narrow cell with memory, sleep, and innumerable recreations of a clipping about a murder in Czechoslovakia.

Once inside the prisoner's dock, however, the atmosphere of the court changes. Although the blinds are down, light filters through them and the air becomes "stiflingly hot," especially since the windows are closed. Only then does Meursault see the row of faces opposite him. Earlier he had considered that he would be "witnessing" a trial; now he is confronted with the prospective jurors, who will be witnessing his trial, listening to witnesses for and against Meursault. But, like the Arab, they are nameless, almost faceless; at this point, they are merely a body of people. He does not comprehend that they are individuals with names and private lives and emotions. He is amused at their stares because he realizes that they are looking at him for signs of criminality. He feels the absurdity and the almost comic aspects of the situation, the unreality of his being confronted by strangers, intently analyzing him as an object on display.

Slowly, as he has done on previous occasions, when he becomes too warm, he begins to feel dizzy. Time becomes heavy once more as he finds that he must continue to endure being the focus of attention by a sea of faces that he cannot recognize. Never before has Meursault been such a focal point. Before the murder, he was, we have to suppose, sufficiently ordinary looking that no one took a second glance, either admiringly or disparagingly. He — a nobody — is, suddenly, someone vastly important. The policeman, to the left of Meursault, explains that the newspapers are responsible for the dense, crowded courtroom. He even points out the press reporters sitting at a table, just below the jury box. One journalist knows the policeman and shakes hands, seems friendly and, later wishes Meursault good luck. When Meursault looks out upon the courtroom, he senses that, perhaps, he should not be here, for the people beyond him are exchanging remarks and seem to belong to a club; he feels ill at ease only because he is alone, an outsider, a stranger, or, as he puts it, a "gate-crasher."

Meursault's case, he discovers, is not as simple as he thinks and, we are led to believe, the crowded courtroom is particularly fascinated by Meursault. The journalist friend of the policeman beside Meursault says that because news was scarce, the journalists have been featuring Meursault's murder of the Arab, along with the news and the gossip surrounding the patricide. Thus the amplification has already begun and Meursault has been ignorant of the fact that his name and his murder of the Arab have been written about by journalists. Since the two murder trials are scheduled one after another, they have, by chance, become linked into a grotesque curiosity. One of the correspondents, it is noted, even came from Paris to cover the patricide, but was asked, as long as he was present, to cover the details of Meursault's trial.

All of this is said to Meursault thoughtlessly, and Meursault, in turn, does not understand the interest in himself and his trial, for he almost comments that it was kind of the Parisian reporter to spend time listening to Meursault's trial; but he stops short when he realizes that it would sound silly. The journalist goes back to his colleagues, with another friendly wave of his hand, and the journalists again chatter and laugh together, all seeming "very much at home." Camus is emphasizing the coziness, the sense of comradship on the part of the press, in addition to that of the crowd in order to point out Meursault's feeling of aloneness and the feeling that he is an outsider, a stranger in their midst.

The account of the trial's opening is discussed quickly because Meursault does not understand the legal maneuvering and rules of order and is conscious, mainly, of a single journalist who is eyeing him but betraying no emotion.

Meursault's consciousness of being an outsider in a courtroom linked by a strange common bond disappears as soon as the witness list is called. Raymond, Masson, Salamano, the doorkeeper from the Home, old Pérez (his mother's closest friend), and Marie slowly emerge from the faceless blur of people, standing, then filing out of the room through a side door. Céleste, the owner of a restaurant that Meursault used to enjoy drinking and eating in is the last to leave. And, by chance, Meursault is startled for a moment at the woman who is beside Céleste. It is the robot-woman whom he observed one evening, but Meursault has little time for thinking about her, for his trial begins immediately. With a touch of black humor, Camus has the Judge describe himself as a "sort of umpire," recalling what Camus said about Meursault's being finally condemned because he "wouldn't play the game." The Judge vows to be scrupulously impartial. This is nonsense, as we well know, for no one is able to be impartial, to any great extent, about a death or, in this case, a murder. He closes by citing that the case will be handled "in the spirit of justice," another ironic comment for justice will not enter into Meursault's trial. His trial will not be impartially viewed, argued about, or judged, and his sentence will not be the result of impartial justice.

After a brief reference to the heat and the public fanning themselves with newspapers and the three judges fanning with plaited straw fans, the Judge begins his questioning of Meursault.

Like a child, Meursault is vaguely annoyed that he must once again answer questions about his identity and give particulars about the crime; but he reasons, like a child, that perhaps this might be the best procedure; it would be wrong if the wrong man were on trial. His innocence mocks the idea of justice having begun, for in a sense, Meursault is being tried for a wrong which he committed, and he will be sentenced for the wrong reasons. His attitude, at this point, is as though he is a spectator, viewing himself, reciting names and places which he has done so many times previously. Indeed, even as the Judge questions Meursault about the account of the murder, it is as though another person were answering "Yes, sir," as instructed by his lawyer to do. Instead of listening to the Judge's questions, Meursault allows himself to concentrate on the youngest journalist whose eyes are fixed on him and, at the same time, he notices the little robot-woman.

When the Judge finishes his routine questioning, he launches into matters which he says might seem irrelevant, but which are in his opinion, highly relevant. Remember, at this point, that the Judge promised to be impartial. Thus Meursault is prepared for what he describes as the "odious" matter of his mother's death.

To the questions about his mother, Meursault is very honest. The questions are, to him, simple. He sent her away because there was not enough money for them both and neither he nor his mother was particularly distressed at the parting. Neither he nor his mother, he adds, "expected much of one another" — or anybody else. Therefore, the new condition and the adjustment was easy.

The Prosecutor is quick to take advantage of Meursault's simple explanations. It is easy for Meursault to explain to him that he had no intention of killing the Arab and, as for his carrying a revolver, that was merely a matter of pure chance. This is the truth, we know, because we are certain of the truth of this man's first-person narrative.

The truthfulness of Meursault's explanations helps confirm what he says happened after the Prosecutor has finished. When he says that he couldn't "quite follow what came next," we are sure that he could not. Meursault is easily and often confused. We observed several instances of this in Part One and especially in the first two chapters of Part Two.

The call for adjournment bewilders Meursault, as does his being hustled into the prison van and given a midday meal. He is tired when he is returned to the courtroom, confronting the same faces and starting the trial over again. This is, in a sense, punishment for Meursault, for, in addition to his being tired and disconcerted by the court proceedings, the heat has increased; Meursault is sweating, barely conscious, and now all of the people in the courtroom have fans and everyone is fanning themselves—except the young journalist and the steel-eyed robot-woman.

The evidence against Meursault's rumored callousness is first confirmed by the warden of the Home. He swears that Meursault's mother complained about her son's conduct and that she reproached him for sending her to the Home. Meursault fails to comprehend the importance of what has been uttered to the jury. To him, the warden of the Home has not qualified his answers and, in addition, it is natural for old people in Homes resenting, at one time or another, being sent there. This fact does not surprise or alarm him.

The warden becomes embarrassed when he has to explain, however, Meursault's "calmness." Calm, normally, is a word with positive connotations; here, it is damning as the warden explains that Meursault's calmness consists of not wanting to see his mother's body, not shedding a tear and not even knowing his mother's age. According to the Code, the Judge asks that the warden identify the man so described as the prisoner Meursault. It is a formal question, but one which the Prosecutor relishes. Meursault is riveted now even more tightly into his role of an unfeeling man, a man who could kill in cold blood. Meursault notes the look of triumph on the man's face. It would be foolish for him to burst into tears, but being the focal point of so much hate as he feels bearing upon him, he does want to cry. He has never before sensed such loathing by another person.

The doorkeeper at the Home adds to the warden's damning evidence, adding that Meursault declined to see the corpse, that he smoked cigarettes and slept and even drank coffee with cream. Of course Meursault is "guilty" of that. Those facts are truth. The frightening aspect of this testimony is that Meursault begins to feel guilty and becomes even more aware that he is being condemned on false charges when the doorkeeper is asked to repeat his statements about smoking and about drinking coffee. A heat of indignation encases the courtroom. Guilty as charged, one might say. But the murder of the Arab has scarcely been touched on; little mention is made of Meursault's killing the native. The focus of the trial, thus far and throughout the remainder of the day, will be on Meursault's behavior during the weekend after his mother's burial.

Embarrassment follows the doorkeeper's statement when Meursault's counsel asks the doorkeeper if, in fact, he too did not smoke. He did, he confesses, but he took the cigarette "just out of politeness." Meursault confirms the truth of giving the cigarette, which gives the doorkeeper so much relief from being accused of also smoking that he confesses that it was he who suggested that Meursault have some coffee.

The statements made by old Pérez are even more damning for Meursault, for the old man recounts that he himself fainted during the funeral and speaks of his being "a great friend" of Meursault's mother and that his grief and his shock were so intense during the funeral that he barely noticed Meursault. He also says that he did not see Meursault shed a tear, but he cannot "swear" to such a statement.

Céleste's testimony begins on a positive note; he admits that Meursault was a customer of his and also a friend; when asked whether or not Meursault was a "secretive" sort of man, Céleste answers instead that Meursault "isn't one to waste his breath, like a lot of folks," meaning the Prosecutor. Clearly, he is trying to help Meursault, saying that he paid his bills. When asked about his opinion of the murder, he says that, in his opinion, it was a stroke of bad luck, an accident, and is abruptly dismissed when the Judge observes that this trial is being held for just such reasons: to judge such "accidents."

Marie's testimony is ripe for the Prosecutor as he draws forth that she and Meursault made love the day following Meursault's mother's funeral; in addition, he forces her to confess that they met while swimming and that they attended a movie together before having sex. Then the Prosecutor brings the trial to a halt with a startling silence, following his statement that the movie they attended was "a comedy film." He pleads with the jury to remember, foremost, that the man they are to judge did these three acts on the very day following his mother's funeral.

Marie's tears and pleas for understanding are of no help; she is led away and the hearing continues, with scarcely anyone paying any attention to the testimony of Masson or Salamano. Salamano, like Marie, asks for understanding, but it is obvious that his attempt is as futile as Marie's tears were.

Raymond, the last witness, states that Meursault is innocent. This is a rash statement, but one typical of the volatile Raymond Sintès. One might think that he protests too quickly. He does explain that Meursault had no motive for killing the Arab, that it was he, Raymond, who had the grudge against the Arab. Meursault's presence, he says, on that particular day was due to "pure coincidence." This is true, but the Prosecutor knows a great deal about this murder, for he asks Raymond about Meursault's writing the defaming letter to the dead Arab's sister. To this question, Raymond can answer only that it was mere chance, which gives the Prosecutor an opportunity to chant "chance" and "mere coincidence" as playing much too large a role in the murder. For example, he points out that Meursault did not interfere when Raymond beat up his mistress, that Meursault swore falsely to the police about Raymond, and points out that this man, who states, unequivocally, that Meursault is innocent is well known as a pimp, as a man who makes a living on the prostitution of women. Meursault is, therefore, pinned against a sordid backdrop of prostitution, brutal fights, a liaison of his own, and a perverted "calmness" during his mother's funeral. The Prosecutor describes Meursault as inhuman, a monster, wholly without morals, a man who indulged himself in an orgy following the death of his mother, and killing a man as part of a vendetta for his best friend, a pimp.

When Meursault's lawyer protests that his client is on trial for murder and not for his associations with certain types of friends or matters happening during and after his mother's funeral, there are a few titters from the courtroom audience. When he tries to gain understanding for his client, the lawyer's gestures are awkward and the Prosecutor is fast on his feet to emphasize that the two elements mentioned are the vital link in this case: Meursault is a criminal at heart. And Meursault notices that "these words seemed to take much effect on the jury and the public."

This statement is certainly true, for if it was the doorkeeper who is the blame for Meursault's drinking coffee, he is guilty of defaming Meursault's character, which the Prosecutor is attempting to do also. And, if the doorkeeper is guilty, then Raymond, by extension, is guilty for suggesting that Meursault write the letter, and Marie is guilty for suggesting the comic movie that she and Meursault attended together. But, remember that in each case, Meursault was given a choice; he could have said no. He must now assume the responsibilities for his actions. One cannot define his actions as models of behavior and the Prosecutor is alert to this, damning Meursault's moral sense, logically, but for the wrong reasons. Later, Meursault will be labeled a monster because he disobeys

conventions; that is, he does not "play the game." Clearly this is
the Prosecutor's most valuable weapon against Meursault and he
uses it repeatedly and stunningly.

The first day of the trial finished, Meursault is conscious, first
of all, of a summer evening out-of-doors; later, sitting in the darkness of the truck, memories return to him of things which had mattered, but things which he had never given value to before—sounds
of a town which he had loved, a certain hour of the day, the languid
air, birds calling, and streetcar noises. Once, he was unconsciously
content with life, but he did not know that he was content or that he
was "living"; only now, in this prison of the moving vehicle does he
realize what has been taken away—forever—from him.

CHAPTER IV

Camus has altered the tone of his narrative slowly as Meursault
has, after a fashion, somewhat adjusted to prison life and is now on
trial for his life. In Part One, Meursault reacted either positively or
negatively or was confused by questions and decisions which he
alone could answer or make. Numerous times, the first-person narrative focused on the simplicity of Meursault's reactions. Now,
however, even Meursault is aware of the sense of detachment which
has grown within him. It was especially evident in the last chapter,
and Camus emphasizes it even more in this chapter.

Meursault, for example, is vaguely aware that he is being thoroughly condemned by the Prosecutor, yet he himself senses a new,
far-reaching indifference to his fate. He is intrigued by the trial. He
finds it "interesting," although he is the prisoner who is hearing
himself discussed. He is a focal point and, as almost an afterthought,
he is aware that more is said about *him* than is said about his crime.
Camus' understatements here confirm what we have seen happening in this so-called court of justice. It is, for Meursault, absurd that
both his own lawyer and the Prosecutor have come to almost the
same conclusion after having argued about Meursault's character.
They agree: Meursault is guilty. Meursault's lawyer differs only in
that he raises his arms to heaven and pleads Meursault's guilt with
extenuating circumstances.

Normally, as has been noted, Meursault is a man of few words,
but he finds himself, at the present, eager to speak out, to add more
to his lawyer's defense. This he has been advised not to do and so

he remains silent. To him, it seems as though he has been excluded from the trial entirely and that his fate is to be decided with his having little to do with the matter.

Tide-like, Meursault's fascination with the trial ebbs and recedes; he listens intently, wanting to protest, then drifts away, only half-hearing the vindictive voice of the Prosecutor. Meursault is aware of the Prosecutor's gestures and his elaborate phrases, but even these, he admits, catch only isolated moments of his attention. It is with almost a sense of impatience that Meursault waits for the Prosecutor to continue as he tries to prove to the jury that the murder was obviously premeditated and that it can be summarized as being the "dark workings of a criminal mentality." Camus' ironic sense of comedy is included in the Prosecutor's tirades. For the Prosecutor, the facts of the crime are "as clear as daylight." Recall that when Meursault fired the shots, he was mesmerized by the daylight. But the sun itself was *not* clear; it was thickly clotted by Meursault's mental state. And note also that Camus has the Prosecutor, in another stroke of ironic comment, add that Meursault's criminal mentality might be called the "dark side of this case." The sun, as we have seen, did darken, blinding Meursault, literally and figuratively. It was so intense that Meursault was blinded by the stinging sweat in his eyes, the blurry vision of the Arab, and he was blinded by the enormity of what was happening. As he said in Part One, the trigger of the pistol simply "gave." Meursault's daylight was so blackened by the sun that he was not even conscious of firing the first shot into the Arab.

Camus' having the Prosecutor reiterate the facts of the crime increases our sense of what Meursault must be feeling as he hears again and again the sequence of, for him at least, "chance" events that occurred, culminating in what the Prosecutor describes as "cold blooded murder." Underscoring his summation, the Prosecutor cites Meursault's education, logically proving that the crime was done by a man capable of premeditation. Had Meursault been a simple, passionate man, perhaps he could have killed the Arab in a moment of madness. But, the Prosecutor tells the jury, this is not the case: Meursault had all his faculties and wits about him when he fired the shots and was quite aware of what he was doing. This, we know, is not so. It is, seemingly logical, but it is false. Meursault was totally unaware of what he was doing and, later, the reason why he did it. Even now, he cannot explain why he murdered the Arab and, especially, why he fired the four extra shots. To the Prosecutor, the four extra shots prove that Meursault was being thorough; to this charge, Meursault has no answer, other than knowing that the Prosecutor is wrong.

Meursault admits to himself that he feels little regret; after all, the man whom he shot was a stranger; he was only an Arab, and, to Meursault, the Prosecutor is overdoing the emphasis on Meursault's regret. Camus, here, is placing Meursault in the position of a judge — listening, watching, observing, and making decisions as to justice being done.

Meursault tells us that he is a man incapable of regret. To regret, philosophically, includes in its definition a re-thinking and contemplation about past actions — these do not exist within Meursault. He is a man of present moments and considers only briefly the immediate future and if the future will contain pleasure. He has never looked backward and contemplated the past, and, for this reason, the entire trial has been an enormously new experience for Meursault. He has had to endure re-hearing the past, depicted by the Prosecutor, and by his own counsel, and judging their versions of the past with his own.

The Prosecutor is a thorough villain; Camus is quite clear in his portrayal of the man, parading him and prancing him before the jury as he states that Meursault clearly lacks a soul and although it would be wrong to condemn a man for something that he lacks, it is logical, and just, that justice cannot tolerate the lack of a soul. Logically, therefore, Meursault is a menace to society. And, although he does not say so at the moment, logically, he could conclude that if one is a menace to society, then, for society's sake, that menace should be done away with — burned, executed, or beheaded.

Consider, also, in this chapter that Camus manipulates the Prosecutor's oratory so that when the man is condemning Meursault, he continually refers to the case following Meursault's — the murder of a father by his son. He links, within the consciousness of the jury, the idea that extenuating circumstances are no excuse. A murder is a murder and an execution is a murderer's just reward. He preys upon the jury, trapped in their seats, in order to construe a physical murder of a father by a son with a "moral" murder of a mother by her son.

The Prosecutor adds that when he asks for the death penalty, he has never asked for a capital sentence with so little pain. Because Meursault is heartless, the Prosecutor feels no qualms because, being a religious man, he is following not only his own conscience, but his sacred obligation. He is now dealing with a criminal who lacks a "spark" (a light image, again) of human feeling.

Meursault's reaction is both physical and one of anguish. When the Prosecutor sits down, Meursault is quite overcome, he says, but he is not wholly defeated because of what the Prosecutor has said. Meursault is suffering terribly from the heat, he tells us first, and then adds that he is also amazed at what he has been hearing.

Meursault, given a chance to speak, says briefly that he had no intention of killing the Arab. After the long harangue, the contrast between his defense and the Prosecutor's defamation is striking. Meursault's only defense for his act was "because of the sun." That is all: "because of the sun." Meursault adds that he spoke too quickly and ran his words together; actually, what he said is of little importance for we are sure what the verdict will be.

Court is adjourned and is continued the following day with no hint of what Meursault thought about during the evening as he waited for the trial to resume. Whether or not he has changed during the interval, we see that little has changed when he is brought back into the courtroom. The fans are still waving before the faces of the jury and the speech by the defense seems as endless, if not more so, than that of the Prosecution. Meursault removes himself from the proceedings, as he has done before; in effect, this is what has happened to him, by order of the court. His lawyer has been used, instead of Meursault himself, to explain the murder and its circumstances. This is particularly vivid to Meursault when he realizes that the lawyer is so enthralled in recounting the murder that he becomes confused and says "I killed a man."

Meursault realizes that he is judging his lawyer and he also realizes that the man is not nearly as "talented" as the Prosecutor. This is appallingly evident in the lawyer's failing to summon to the attention of the jury the issue of the trial: Meursault is on trial for killing an Arab—not for his actions at his mother's funeral and certainly not for any of his adventures with Marie and Raymond. In addition, Meursault tells us nothing of his lawyer's defense concerning why Meursault was carrying the gun in the first place. Thus we must assume that the lawyer did not mention the subject. Further, the lawyer fails to grasp the easiest explanation possible for

Meursault's shooting the Arab: Meursault saw that the Arab had a knife; the initial shot was fired in self-defense and the ensuing shots were fired because of panic and fright. This makes absolutely good sense and is logical and carries sufficient persuasiveness that the jury probably would accept the truth of such statements. But such explanations are not even brought to their attention. At times, therefore, Meursault's lawyer seems to be a dolt, feeble and ridiculous, especially when he counters the Prosecutor's arguments concerning Meursault's soul.

To our dismay, we listen to him return to the matter, once more, of Meursault's mother. This is rhetorical quicksand, a subject that has engulfed the entire trial and has been given a thorough damnation by the Prosecutor. The defense says proudly that such institutions as the Home are excellent and are promoted and financed by the government. His logic is absurd: Meursault's soul exists because he was sufficiently humane to put his mother into a "government" Home.

It seems, at times, that Meursault can bear hearing no more, for not only can he not defend himself, he cannot explain his actions. The repetitious recreation of the past sickens him; he feels as though he could vomit because of the rush of memories flooding over him. And, in his remembering, consider that Meursault remembers the physical, not the philosophical, aspects of scenes — the warm smells, the color of the sky at evening, the feel of Marie's dress, and the sound of her laughter. These sensations are denied to him and never before has Meursault been confronted with the disappearance of an entire world. Formerly, his life was composed of warm skies, swimming, and sex, and little thought was given to one day following another and the disappearence, forever, of present moments that he was delighting in.

The trial over, Meursault is so exhausted that he utters a naked, blatant lie; he says that his defense has been fine. His insincerity troubles him a bit, but he is far too tired to judge whether or not it could be labeled, decisively, "fine." Ironically, we pause and consider that had Meursault "played the game" — had he wept during the trial, wrung his hands, exhibited any emotion or remorse, the Prosecutor's case would have failed.

Even Marie's presence cannot rouse Meursault now from his stupor as he awaits the verdict. He reveals that he feels as though his heart had "turned to stone," leaving us with an ironic affirmation that Meursault is, indeed, heartless.

When he hears that he is to be decapitated in "some public place," he says that he sensed a respectful sympathy within the courtroom and then he "stopped thinking altogether." We do not; we cannot. We continue thinking and questioning the justness of such a verdict.

CHAPTER V

At the beginning of this chapter, Meursault very briefly notes that he has refused to see the prison chaplain for the third time; then he dismisses the subject as quickly as he dismissed the chaplain, and turns to another subject. He speaks of hope. There has been an element of hope within him despite his knowledge that death is a soon certainty, and caught between his hope for life and his certainty of death, Meursault's thoughts have become wild and random. He grasps for the impossible: freedom *must* be possible, he thinks, if for no other reason than that of chance. (Remember that chance is largely responsible for his being in prison.) He remarks that had he —just once—read an escape story and discovered at least one instance in which chance saved a man from execution, he would be satisfied. But he cannot cling to hope for long, and so these paragraphs of doubt and hope counterpoint one another. As soon as Meursault envisions the possibility of escape, he confronts himself with the fact that he is caught in "a rattrap, irrevocably." The ebb and flow of his contrasting emotions are evocative of the movement of the sea, yet they resemble more the intake and gasping for breath of a drowning man.

Even one of Meursault's former consolations is of little comfort to him now. Earlier, Meursault imagined being imprisoned within a tree, able to see only a piece of sky; in his new cell, he can, in fact, see nothing but the sky, but circumstances have changed. His punishment now is not mere imprisonment. Here he must face not an endless punishment; he must cope every morning with the fear of hearing footsteps, the prelude to his beheading. Prisoners in Algiers are never told when they are to be executed; thus Meursault has no opportunity to adjust for an eternity of punishment as, for example, Sisyphus had.

These desperate moments of hope, of escape, flow through a mind that cannot fathom fully, with certitude, that this imprisonment, this waiting to be killed, is happening to him—a nobody of a person, a clerk, a man who has asked nothing from life other than a few pleasures and that he be left alone. It is probably impossible for Meursault, as it would be for any man, to fully realize death's nothingness. For this reason, Meursault's imagination is released and allowed free rein to comfort him. Formerly, imagination was of no use to Meursault. His life consisted of whatever was occurring to him at any given moment. His current "present" however is unbearable and so he must find an alternative, another way of existing, moment to moment, as he awaits the certain, yet unknown, dawn when he will be led to the guillotine.

Even Meursault's imagination fails, though, for the most part, because he is basically a practical man. He cannot even romanticize that he will ascend majestically a flight of stairsteps above a crowd of people awaiting his beheading. He remembers, oddly, in this chapter, some things his mother used to tell him—some old, philosophical homilies, but because he has always lived without much forethought or hindsight, his agony is scarcely relieved by remembering his mother's platitudes. Clearly, Meursault is able to measure his own degree of panic. He is frightened and repelled by his thoughts of dying and he realizes at the same time how absurd such panic is. Man must eventually die and, in addition, the world will continue—without any man, many men, and certainly without Meursault.

It is interesting that Meursault refuses "to play *the* game" by seeing the chaplain, confessing his sins and asking for prayers and consolation. Yet he allows his imagination to play *a* game with chance and possibility. At the same time, he keeps, with effort, some control on his thoughts, for he knows that his execution is probably inevitable. But is there an alternative? Perhaps he can appeal, successfully. He sustains himself by thinking, constantly thinking: if he is able to maintain control over his thoughts, he can gain some semblance of peace of mind.

But his peace of mind, even if achieved, is brief. His thoughts return too quickly to a familiar groove—to Marie—and he considers her feelings about being labeled the mistress of a man who murdered another man; she is the mistress of a man who is sentenced to die. He wonders about her. She is alive now. If she were to die, her memories of Meursault die also. And, if she is dead, and once Meursault is dead, he will be absolutely forgotten. No trace of him will remain, even in a memory.

When the prison chaplain walks in, unannounced, Meursault's

shock is evident. He has been caught off guard: he has been caught thinking. One senses that Meursault has been surprised when he is naked; he is vulnerable, for normally he clothes himself in indifference, passivity, or physical activity.

Meursault describes the chaplain's behavior as an attempt to be friendly, and he describes the chaplain, himself, as a mild, amiable man. Knowing that the chaplain has not come to offer last words, the quiet within the cell allows Meursault to drift outside himself, observing the chaplain's eyes, his knees, and his sinewy hands. Meursault is a master at this kind of observation, admitting that for awhile he almost forgets that the chaplain is there, a live human being, sitting on Meursault's bed. Like the examining magistrate, the chaplain cannot accept Meursault's statement that God does not exist; he has come to Meursault's cell to assure him that his doubts about God are too certain and, therefore, might be wrong. When he questions Meursault about a belief being too thorough and the possibility that the reverse is true, Meursault answers that the chaplain may be right, but, most of all, Meursault is sure that he is *not* interested in discussing God.

The chaplain is unwilling to accept Meursault's lack of spiritual interest, saying that Meursault's feelings are fostered because of desperation, which, we realize, is most unlikely. Meursault feels fear — not desperation; in fact, he lacks the time to even begin a discussion about God because any discussion of God would involve sin and guilt and, although Meursault has been pronounced guilty, he emphatically does not accept that guilt. He also refuses to be consoled with the chaplain's observation that "all men are under a sentence of death." Meursault has already considered this notion himself and it is futile to philosophize about "death" and "all men." Meursault is undaunted by the chaplain's standing suddenly and sternly staring him in the eyes; it is, he says, a trick he himself has played.

Meursault drifts away as the chaplain laments about the suffering of a man who does not believe in an afterlife; he is roused only when the chaplain becomes so agitated that he professes a belief in the possibility that Meursault's appeal will succeed. Meursault is convinced that he has *not* sinned: a man of God has no business in his cell. He committed a criminal offense, not a sin, and God's laws should have no dimension in civil matters. He may be guilty of a civil offense but he is not guilty of sinning. Meursault is incapable of imagining the face of God on the stone walls, as the chaplain suggests. He wants only to conjure, before him, Marie's face, "sun-gold, lit up with desire."

Like the examining magistrate, the formerly "mild, amiable" man is metamorphosed into a madman, swinging around and crying out in defiance against Meursault's staunch refusal to believe in an afterlife.

In contrast, Meursault is calm and bored; of course he knows that one might wish, perhaps at times, for an afterlife, but such wishes are a waste of time. Man cannot change death's being an eternal void.

Meursault's request that the chaplain leave is not granted. The man is determined to squeeze out of Meursault some piece of his humanity that *must* be spiritual—which, in a sense, he does manage to accomplish. Meursault's imagination *can* picture an afterlife, but only an afterlife in which he can remember this life on earth. For Meursault, a spiritual existence is absolutely impossible unless it consists of a mind, residing in eternity, and doing one thing: remembering the pleasure of a man's former, physical life. Meursault has no use for any spiritual "present" moments in a vaporous spiritual world. Meursault is an active, physical man and the constant memory of such things as swimming and sex is the only kind of an afterlife possible for him.

When the chaplain begins to pray, Meursault is transformed into a madman himself, yelling, hurling insults, and grabbing the chaplain by the neckband of his cassock. He is desperate; he has precious few moments left to him and yet he is still being punished, even now, by a man who wants to be called Father and who wants to pray for his "son." Meursault describes his joy and rage as he attacks the certainty of the chaplain's beliefs; none of this man's spiritual certainties is comparable to a physical strand of a woman's hair. The only certainty important at this moment is the surety of Meursault's pending death, and his mind reels as his hands tighten on the chaplain. Meursault is so wrought with rage that several jailers finally have to rescue the chaplain.

Afterward, in the calm of the night, Meursault is able to fall asleep, until just before daybreak; then he is flooded by smells and sounds, physical responses during what he fears might be his last moments on earth. The sound of a steamer reminds him of his anonymity; not a single person on the boat knows or cares about

Meursault's fate, and it is at that moment that he understands the odd behavior of his mother as she approached death. She succumbed to a game of sorts, playing as though she were young once more, delighting in the interest that Old Pérez offered to her. Pérez cared.

Meursault realizes that his mother rebelled against dying. She "played" at beginning again. Likewise, so will Meursault. At last he is drained. He is emptied of all hope. And he is free. He can face the universe, alone — without fearing any man or any god. The "benign indifference" of the universe is no threat to him. He is, at last, able to defy everything and everybody because he has gained the knowledge that his indifference is akin to that of the universe. He is not to be pitied because he is a victim of a prejudiced jury. He has determined his own value to himself and, in addition, has realized an entirely new sense of self value: he knows how deeply his indifference and disbelief disturb society. One must "play the game" if he is to live within society. But in order to do this, one must give up being absolutely true to himself and acting according to his conscience. Society cannot afford to harbor strangers or outsiders who live by other rules. Society demands obedience. Meursault cannot be subservient to the emotional mores of the Algerian masses. Meursault's truth is his only companion, and he will die, defending his right *not* to cry at his mother's funeral and his right *not* to profess a belief in God. What good is it to attempt tears or swear beliefs in the name of truth when they would be melodramatically fraudulent?

Meursault has confronted the absurdity of his life and of life itself. In Part One, he lived without pausing to consider the meaning of his present moments, his past, or his future. He was either satisfied, or content, or bored. He placed no emphasis on his life's significance. Now, he realizes that the universe and most of the world are indifferent to his fate. So he *will* play the game of the Absurd; he himself will live as long as he can — giving his life *his* meaning, even though he knows that ultimately, it has no meaning. He will watch and measure his life's meaning as he faces what he hopes to be a howling mob. If he is so hated and such a threat to that mob of people, he will be able to laugh at their fear of him. He does not fear their hatred. He can determine the extent of his importance by measuring how thoroughly he is a threat to them. Meursault can imagine dying, enjoying the absurdity of his rejection. The crowd that howls for his blood are *not* free; they have not been forced to question their existence. They are governed and bound by secular and sacred laws which Meursault will not accept. He realizes that nothing—no value—is lasting or eternal. His former indifference was mute; now he can articulate and justify his new indifference and, with this insight, he is able to attain ecstatic peace.

CHARACTER ANALYSES

Meursault

Because so much time has been spent throughout the discussion of this novel, analyzing Meursault's character, there is little elaboration that would be more than speculation. Basically, one should remember that Meursault is a man who will not lie about himself, a man who cannot accept the formulas by which his society convinces itself it is happy. He will not look forward to a life after death, he will not use religion as a vehicle to avoid facing the fact that he must die, and he refuses to mask his calm acceptance of his mother's death. He defies all judges, except himself: he will not play the hypocritical penitent for his interrogators and prosecutors.

Perhaps one of the most valuable ways to understand Meursault is to quote what Camus has said about him:

"Meursault for me," writes Camus, is "a poor and naked man, in love with the sun which leaves no shadows. He is far from being totally deprived of sensitivity for he is animated by a passion, profound because it is tacit, the passion for the absolute and for truth. It is still a negative truth, the truth of being and feeling, but a truth without which no conquest of the self or of the world is possible." That is why, until the very end, "Meursault is the man who answers but never asks a question, and all his answers so alarm a society which cannot bear to look at the truth."

Marie

The few clues that we have about Marie's personality come from Meursault and he is not given to analyzing himself or other people and so we know little other than she seems, basically, an uncomplicated middle-class young woman. She wants marriage, children, enjoys casual sex, swimming, movies, and outings to the beach. She is frightened and terrified when Meursault is arrested; her life, one would guess, has never been confronted with such drama. Like Meursault, she has had rather unimportant jobs; he is a clerk, she was a typist. She is attracted to Meursault because he enjoys many things that she does and also because he is a little "different." When Meursault agrees to marry her, Marie is happy. Meursault will probably be an adequate husband; he will probably have a steady job, an income that she needn't worry about, and she doesn't ask much more from a man. Like Meursault, she does not demand much from life or from other people.

Marie is on the fringe of this novel, even though Meursault has agreed to marry her. But one should remember that she had great hope for her new life in Paris with Meursault. She is much more of a romantic than he is. She has her daydreams and is happier than we have ever seen her. When Meursault is arrested and sentenced to death, her dreams also die. Later, she is obscured by Meursault's introspection and she drifts away, from the plot, from Meursault, to everyday life and everyday routine.

Raymond

Even before we see Raymond in action we can infer a great deal about his personality. He is short and thick-set and has a flattened nose. He wears flashy clothes, but his room is unclean and the walls are covered by pinup pictures. His reputation as a pimp never is much of a problem for him; most of his friends are pumps, except Meursault and Masson. He repeatedly seeks reassurance, usually by violence, and thus we can be fairly sure that his macho pose is just a front for insecurity. He struts, is a tough guy, but isn't intelligent enough to realize how easily even Meursault sees through his veneer. He is humiliated more than physically harmed when he is wounded by the Arab's knife. He is not a close friend of Meursault; Meursault simply has no objection to spending time in the evenings with Raymond, sharing wine and food and listening to Raymond rant about the newest crisis in his life. And yet Meursault stands trial for a crime that Raymond may well have committed had Meursault not gone to the beach that particular Sunday.

REVIEW QUESTIONS

1. Meursault is a Frenchman living in Algeria; of what importance is this fact?
2. Describe the wake and the funeral of Meursault's mother, detailing Meursault's reactions and impressions.
3. The sun is a complex symbol in this novel. Describe the dual role that it plays, noting particularly the role in the climactic murder.
4. Discuss Camus' literary style in *The Stranger*.
5. How does Camus employ cause-and-effect in this novel?
6. In terms of Camus' philosophy of the Absurd, of what significance is the prison?
7. Why does Meursault place such a high value on the sea? What does it mean to him?
8. How would you have defended Meursault?
9. Compare the judicial character of the examining magistrate and the spiritual character of the priest.
10. Relate Meursault's interest in the robot-woman to his scrapbooks. How does his interest in her help us understand more about him?
11. What role does hope play in the second half of the novel?
12. What is Meursault's idea of an afterlife?
13. Evaluate the justice that was accorded Meursault during his trial and his sentencing.
14. Which played the greater role—emotion or reason—during Meursault's trial? In what way was each employed?
15. Explain Meursault's passivity during his interrogation and imprisonment.
16. Describe Meursault's moment of genuine revolt.
17. Do you think that Meursault is capable of love?
18. Meursault is often characterized as a man who makes no choices. Yet Meursault makes a single very important choice. What is it?
19. Contrast Meursault's view of society with society's expectations of Meursault.
20. How does *The Myth of Sisyphus* explore and expand the significance of *The Stranger?*

SELECTED BIBLIOGRAPHY

Abel, Lionel. "Albert Camus, Moralist of Feeling," *Commentary*, Vol. 31, No. 2 (Feb. 1961), pp. 172-75.

Barnes, Hazel E. *Humanistic Existentialism: The Literature of Possibility*. Lincoln, Nebraska: University of Nebraska Press. 1962.

Beebe, Maurice. "Criticism of Albert Camus: A Selected Checklist of Studies in English," *Modern Fiction Studies*, Vol. 10, No. 3 (Autumn 1964), pp. 303-14.

Bittner, William. "The Death of Camus," *Atlantic Monthly*, Vol. 207, No. 2 (Feb. 1961), pp. 85-88.

Brearley, Katherine. "The Theme of Isolation in Camus," *Kentucky Foreign Language Quarterly*, Vol. 9, No. 3 (1962), pp. 117-22.

Brée, Germaine. "Introduction to Albert Camus," *French Studies*, Vol. 4, No. 1 (Jan. 1950), pp. 27-37.

_____. *Camus*. New Brunswick: Rutgers University Press. 1959.

_____. "The Genesis of *The Stranger*," *Shenandoah*, Vol. 12, No. 3 (Spring 1961), pp. 3-10.

Bruckberger, Raymond-Leopold. "The Spiritual Agony of Europe," *Renascence*, VII, No. 2 (Winter 1954), pp. 70-80.

Cruickshank, John. *Albert Camus and the Literature of Revolt*. London: Oxford University Press. 1959.

Frank, Waldo. "Life in the Face of Absurdity," *New Republic*, CXXXIII, No. 12 (Sept. 19, 1955), pp. 18-20.

Frohock, W. M. "Camus: Image, Influence, and Sensibility," *Yale French Studies*, II, No. 2 (Fourth Study), pp. 91-99.

Gershman, Herbert S. "On *L'Etranger*," *French Review*, XXIX, No. 4 (Feb. 1956), pp. 299-305.

Hanna, Thomas. *The Thought and Art of Albert Camus*. Chicago: Henry Regnery Co. 1958.

Harrington, Michael. "The Despair and Hope of Modern Man," *Commonweal*, LXIII, No. 2 (Oct. 1956), pp. 224-33.

John, S. "Image and Symbol in the Work of Albert Camus," *French Studies*, IX, No. 1 (Jan. 1955), pp. 42-53.

King, Adele. *Camus*. London: Oliver and Boyd. 1964.

Mason, H. A. "M. Camus and the Tragic Hero," *Scrutiny*, XIV, No. 2 (Dec. 1946), pp. 82-89.

Rolo, Charles. "Albert Camus: A Good Man," *Atlantic*, Vol. 201, No. 5 (May 1958), pp. 27-33.

Scott, Nathan H. *Albert Camus*. London: Bowes and Bowes. 1962.

Theody, Philip. *Albert Camus: A Study of his Works*. London: Hamish Hamilton. 1957.

Viggiani, Carl A. "Camus in 1936: The Beginnings of a Career," *Symposium*, Vol. 12, Nos. 1-2 (Spring-Fall 1958), pp. 7-18.

_____. "Camus' *L'Etranger*," *PMLA*, Vol. 71, No. 5 (Dec. 1956), pp. 865-87.

NOTES

NOTES